Eat to Defeat Menopause

ALSO BY KAREN GIBLIN

Manual of Management Counseling for the Perimenopausal and Menopausal Patient: A Clinician's Guide (Written with Mary Jane Minkin, MD)

ALSO BY MACHE SEIBEL, MD

The Soy Solution for Menopause: An Alternative to Estrogen (Author)

Infertility: A Comprehensive Text (Editor)

Technology and Infertility: Clinical, Psychosocial, Legal and Ethical Aspects (Edited with Ann Kiessling and Judith Bernstein)

Infertility: Your Questions Answered (Written with Howard S. Jacobs and S. L. Tan)

Family Building through Egg and Sperm Donation (Written with Susan L. Crockin)

Ovulation Induction (Edited with Richard E. Blackwell, MD)

Infertility: A Comprehensive Text, 2nd Edition (Editor)

Infertility: Your Questions Answered, 2nd Edition (Written with Howard S. Jacobs and S. L. Tan)

A Woman's Book of Yoga: Embracing Our Natural Life Cycles (Written with Hari Kaur Khalsa)

Journal Babies: Your Personal Conception and Pregnancy Organizer (Written with J. Stephenson)

Eat to Defeat Menopause

RECIPES FOR A HEALTHY MIDLIFE

Dear Dolores,
The greatest love of all is for the love of food.
Wishing you good health and happiness.

With affection,

Karen Giblin

A Red Hot Mamas® / HealthRock® Book

Karen Giblin & Mache Seibel, MD

Published by Red Hot Mamas Publishing
    7712 Georgetown Chase
    Roswell, GA 30075
    www.redhotmamas.org

ISBN: 978-0-615-31803-5

10 9 8 7 6 5 4 3 2 1

Printed in Canada.

All product/brand names are trademarks or registered trademarks of their respective trademark holders.

Cover illustration and design: Darren Wheeling, Black Egg Syndicate

Disclaimer: We have taken care to ensure that the information in this book is accurate. However, we can give no absolute guarantees as to the accuracy or completeness of the content of this book. We accept no liability for any losses or damages (whether direct, indirect, special, consequential, or otherwise) arising out of errors or omissions contained in this book.

Callawind
Custom Cookbooks
Produced by Callawind Custom Cookbooks
(a division of Callawind Publications Inc.)
3551 St. Charles Boulevard, Suite 179
Kirkland, Quebec H9H 3C4
info@callawind.com | www.callawind.com

Book design: Marcy Claman
Editing: Andrea Lemieux
Indexing: Heather Ebbs

CONTENTS

Many people tend to think of breakthroughs in medicine as a new drug, laser, or high-tech surgical procedure. They often have a hard time believing that the simple choices we make in our lifestyle—what we eat, how we respond to stress, whether or not we smoke, how much exercise we get, and the quality of our relationships and social support—can be as powerful as drugs and surgery, but they often are. Often, even better.

For more than 30 years, I have directed a series of studies showing what a powerful difference changes in diet and lifestyle can make. My colleagues and I at the non-profit Preventive Medicine Research Institute showed, for the first time, that many diseases, including heart disease, prostate cancer, diabetes, and hypertension are often reversible, and thus largely preventable.

We used high-tech, state-of-the-art measures to prove the power of simple, low-tech, and low-cost interventions. We showed that integrative medicine approaches may stop or even reverse the progression of coronary heart disease, diabetes, hypertension, obesity, hypercholesterolemia, and other chronic conditions. We also published the first randomized controlled trial showing that these lifestyle changes may slow, stop, or even reverse the progression of prostate cancer, and may affect breast cancer as well.

Our latest research shows that changing lifestyle changes our genes in only three months—turning on hundreds of genes that prevent disease and turning off genes and oncogenes associated with breast cancer and prostate cancer, as well as genes that cause heart disease, oxidative stress, and inflammation. We also found that these lifestyle changes increase telomerase, the enzyme that lengthens telomeres, the ends of our chromosomes that control how long we live. Even drugs have not been shown to do this.

Although it's understandable that many people feel more bewildered than ever when they hear seemingly contradictory advice about different diets, there is actually a convergence of recommendations that is evolving. Although some significant differences remain, there is an emerging consensus among nutrition experts about what constitutes a healthy way of eating and living. It looks a lot like what you find in this book.

What you *include* in your diet is as important as what you *exclude.* There are at least 100,000 substances in foods that have powerful anticancer, anti–heart disease, and antiaging properties. These include phytochemicals, bioflavonoids, carotenoids, retinols, isoflavones, genistein, lycopene, polyphenols, and so on.

Where do you find these potent substances? With few exceptions, these protective·factors are found in fruits, vegetables, whole grains, legumes, soy products, and in some fish. These are rich in good carbs, good fats, good proteins, and other protective substances. The recipes in this book are high in these protective substances.

You have a spectrum of choices. In all of our studies, we found that the more you change your lifestyle, and the more things you change, the better you feel and the healthier you become. And the better you feel, the easier it is to maintain these changes. Sustainable changes are based on joy, pleasure, and freedom, not deprivation and austerity.

It's not just about preventing illness or living *longer;* it's about living *better.* These lifestyle changes are likely to make you feel so much better, so quickly, that it reframes the reason for changing from fear of dying to joy of living.

When you eat and live healthier, your brain gets more blood so you think more clearly, have more energy, need less sleep. You can even grow so many new brain cells that your brain can get measurably bigger in just a few months! Your skin gets more blood so you wrinkle less and look younger. Your sexual organs get more blood flow in the same way that drugs like Viagra work, so you enhance sexual potency.

Now, *Eat to Defeat Menopause* describes how these same lifestyle changes can help empower and address the needs of menopausal women.

Dr. Seibel is a national expert in menopause and Director of the Complicated Menopause Program at the University of Massachusetts Medical School, where he is also a professor. That, along with his books on soy, *The Soy Solution for Menopause,* and yoga, *A Woman's Book of Yoga,* provide him the wisdom and experience to offer readers much needed information. Karen Giblin founded Red Hot Mamas Menopause Education Programs in 1991. These programs are held in hospitals within the US and Canada. She has conducted numerous research projects and is nationally recognized for her work in women's health. They have combined health information and recipes to help women on their journey through menopause.

The selections in this cookbook are from the authors and from chefs across the United States. The information on menopause and recipes in this book should be of great help to women as they search for easy-to-understand information about this sacred and transformative stage of life. I hope you find it to be useful.

Dean Ornish, MD
Founder and President, Preventive Medicine Research Institute
Clinical Professor of Medicine, University of California, San Francisco
Author, *The Spectrum*

ACKNOWLEDGMENTS

Just as many wonderful flavors and ingredients contribute to a great recipe, many wonderful people contributed to this cookbook. First, we would like to thank our spouses, Drs. Hjalmar Lagast and Sharon Seibel for their encouragement and assistance, and for allowing us to spend hours of family time to work on this project. We also want to thank the many chefs and contributors who provided healthy, delicious recipes to help women *Eat to Defeat Menopause*.

Rachel Giblin and Cynthia Niles worked tirelessly to coordinate this book and bring it together. Thank you to Marcy Claman of Callawind Publications for her pleasant persistence in producing this high-quality book in a timely way. Andrea Lemieux did a fabulous job of editing the content. We would like to offer a special thanks to Barbara Olendzki, RD, MPH, the Nutrition Program Director of the Preventive and Behavior Medicine Department of the University of Massachusetts Medical School and her associate Vijayalakshmi Patil, MS, RD, who ensured that the recipes were not only delicious, but also calorie and fat conscious, and complied with the Department of Health and Human Services recommendations. Thanks to Paul Pillat for helping with the distribution of this book, Darren Wheeling of Black Egg Syndicate for his beautiful illustrations, and to Karen Bressler, CEO of Agar Foods, who helped identify a number of the chefs who contributed. We also want to thank Dan Zaccagnini for his introduction to former White House Chef Will Greenwood, and Allison Gallaher for her administrative efforts. In addition, we want to thank Dr. Dean Ornish, not only for providing the foreword to our book, but also for being an inspiration and teacher of healthy eating to us all.

Because we realize that not everyone in America has the opportunity to have nutritious meals every day, we are donating a portion of the proceeds from our book to three charities: Meals on Wheels, the Greater Boston Food Bank, and Community Servings of Boston.

This is a special hello and welcome from the ethnic kitchens of two people whose day jobs are dealing with menopausal health and education. One kitchen is Italian-American and the other Jewish-American. And we have surprises and great recipes that *la famiglia* (Italian for family) and *mishpokhe* (Yiddish for family) alike will enjoy. It will also help them have healthier families and may help the women improve their menopause symptoms.

I (Karen Giblin) grew up in an Italian-American family, and that meant lots of love and lots of food and lots of food to love. My family actually brought over the first pizza recipe to Baltimore. They owned an Italian bakery and a well-known restaurant in a section of Baltimore called "Little Italy." The restaurant was called "DeNitti's." Of course, I was always told, "Eat this, it's good, and it's good for you!" I love to cook. And, yes indeed, to eat. And now I want to share my simply delicious Italian collection of mouthwatering healthy recipes. And since I had a surgical menopause, I later founded the Red Hot Mamas, the largest menopause education management organization in this country and Canada, which provides women information—to arm them with knowledge—about the changes associated with the menopausal years. My website, www.redhotmamas.org, provides medically sound and valuable information to women across the world. I now want to go a step further and share some of my family recipes that provide better health and may lower the symptoms of menopause. I know for a fact that you can eat Italian meals, including a wonderful bowl of pasta, and enjoy every bite. However, you cannot eat pasta in unlimited amounts. In Italy, menopausal women are not fat, they're just super hot. And by hot, I mean that they have fabulous bodies at all ages. And forget the food adage that says, "Food that's good for you can't taste good." It's a myth. Our recipes prove that you can actually eat food that tastes good, *and* it will be good for you and your family.

I (Mache Seibel) grew up in a Jewish-American family where there was great food and continuous music. I spent some of my favorite time in Bubbie's (Yiddish for grandma) kitchen as assistant chef and chief taster for recipes now known as "bubbielicious." The house became a magnet for family and friends because there was always good company, inviting music, and delicious food waiting. I was always told, "Eat this, it's good, and it's good for you!" As Bubbie entered menopause (shhhh . . . she's not talking age), she found even healthier ways to keep the same great taste. I learned to translate "a handful of this" and "a pinch of that" into fabulous recipes that are both healthy and nutritious. I also went to medical school, trained at Harvard, and became an expert in menopause, soy, and women's health. I founded HealthRock® to use music and songs to make health education fun and memorable—like Schoolhouse Rock, but for health. My websites, www.healthrock.com and www.healthrockwomen.com, have songs on health, wellness, and nutrition that are useful for menopausal women (and some of them are referenced in this cookbook). Now I want to share my healthy, delicious recipes and tell you why they're good for you. The companion CD, *Recipe for Relaxation: Music for Body and Soul,* was created for all you Red Hot Mamas to chill and relax with while you cook and eat to defeat menopause.

We would like to dedicate this book to our mothers, who taught us the importance of a healthy diet and made us realize that the main difference between an Italian mother and a Jewish mother is how they make the sauce, and to our children who have been taught to "eat this, it's good, and it's good for you!"

We hope you enjoy our book!

NO ILLNESS WHICH CAN BE TREATED BY DIET SHOULD BE
TREATED BY ANY OTHER MEANS.
—*Moses Maimonides, AD 1200*

This cookbook is for the Red Hot Mamas of the world. Yes,
you! There are approximately 50 million of you in the United
States alone. You are in or near menopause and you want to
live long and be strong. And the best way to do that is to make
wiser food choices, exercise, and watch your weight. That's
important, since nearly one-third of adults are obese and have
a body mass index (BMI) of 30 or greater. Menopausal women
need between 1,800 and 2,200 calories per day, depending on
their level of activity (see below). We want you to get the most
from your calories by eating delicious and nutritious food so
you eat healthy and don't gain weight.

There are special nutritional needs of women in their
menopausal years. Some of the physical changes that occur
are oftentimes inevitable. However, some of these changes
may be due to bad habits that may not only make menopausal
symptoms worse, but they may also rob women of good health
at menopause and beyond. And for the *mamas* and *bubbies*
who enjoy cooking, our recipes are good for the whole family
and are designed to introduce you to the world of delicious,
healthy eating.

Eating well and exercising may take time and effort, and many
women are at a loss as to where to begin. Our book offers a
variety of suggestions on how to confidently prepare healthy
foods that may affect the symptoms of menopause as well as
different aspects of health. In essence, we show you how to
eat healthy and stay healthy.

WHY WE WROTE THIS COOKBOOK

This cookbook is a little different from most cookbooks. This first section you're about to read has information about menopause. It also has some Red Hot Tips we think will be particularly helpful. We've provided useful tables and charts, "factoids" and "fictionoids," and foods to say *yes* to and foods to say *no* to, among other things. And, we may be the only cookbook to recommend a song to emphasize a key health message.

Eat to Defeat Menopause won't tell you how to exercise, though it will help you exercise good judgment to make the best food choices. It will give you the basic health and nutrition information you need so you can live long and stay healthy and strong. In addition to some great recipes we will give you from our own kitchens, we've also asked chefs from some of America's favorite restaurants to share some of their healthiest, delicious recipes to offer you an even wider range of wonderful choices.

This is not a hot-flash cookbook, though some of the recipes will help to reduce hot flashes. But the ideas and recipes are not a flash in the pan. It's not a soy book like *The Soy Solution for Menopause*;[1] *Eat to Defeat Menopause* is a cookbook of healthy and delicious recipes created for you Red Hot Mamas. Read the text to learn about menopause, healthy eating, and nutrition tips. Use the recipes to have delicious meals that will be heart healthy, help you watch your weight, and may even help you reduce hot flashes. You'll also impress your friends and family because you will not only be a Red Hot Mama—you'll be a Red Hot Chef as well! Take the pause out of menopause, enjoy life, and thank you for letting us introduce you to the world of healthy and delicious eating. Eat to defeat menopause!

THERE IS NO SINCERER LOVE THAN THE LOVE OF FOOD.
—*George Bernard Shaw*

WOMEN AND WEIGHT GAIN

Weight gain is, well, a huge topic, especially in perimenopause and menopause. Hormonal changes may suddenly cause a woman's once curvy hourglass or pear-shaped figure to become more apple-shaped. It happens in part because lower estrogen levels can trigger fat to shift to the center of the body and accumulate around the belly. We've heard women describe this as "swelly bellies." A larger waist increases your chances of getting diabetes, high blood pressure, and heart disease. Are you at increased risk? Measure your waist just above your belly button. A healthy waist measurement is less than 35 inches for a woman (less than 40 inches for a man), assuming your body mass index (BMI, see below) is less than 25.

We can't blame all of this on hormonal changes. Two major culprits are poor eating habits and lack of exercise. The good news is you can rethink how you eat and eat to promote good health, shed some pounds, and focus on putting fitness back into your life.

DON'T WAIT TO LOSE WEIGHT

Losing weight is a simple concept—just eat fewer calories than your body uses. You can do that by eating healthy, controlling the size of your portions, exercising to burn more calories, or a combination of all three. Let this cookbook be your guide.

This isn't a diet book. But if you stick with the recipes and information in this cookbook, you have a good chance of losing weight. And that's important. People in the United States and other industrialized countries are gaining 1 to 2 pounds per year. A survey by American Sports Data found that 3.8 million people in the United States weigh more than 300 pounds, 400,000 people (mostly men) weigh more than 400 pounds, and the average adult female weighs 163 pounds, which is 20 to 30 pounds overweight, depending on height. According to a report by the US Surgeon General, obesity causes 300,000 deaths every year. Some people are literally eating themselves to death!

TABLE 1. ESTIMATED CALORIE REQUIREMENTS (IN KILOCALORIES) FOR EACH GENDER AND AGE GROUP AT THREE LEVELS OF PHYSICAL ACTIVITY[a,2]

Estimated amounts of calories needed to maintain energy balance for various gender and age groups at three different levels of physical activity. The estimates are rounded to the nearest 200 calories and were determined using the Institute of Medicine equation.

| Gender | Age (years) | Activity Level [b,c,d] | | |
		Sedentary[b]	Moderately Active[c]	Active[d]
Child	2–3	1,000	1,000–1,400[e]	1,000–1,400[e]
Female	4–8	1,200	1,400–1,600	1,400–1,800
	9–13	1,600	1,600–2,000	1,800–2,200
	14–18	1,800	2,000	2,400
	19–30	2,000	2,000–2,200	2,400
	31–50	1,800	2,000	2,200
	51+	1,600	1,800	2,000–2,200
Male	4–8	1,400	1,400–1,600	1,600–2,000
	9–13	1,800	1,800–2,200	2,000–2,600
	14–18	2,200	2,400–2,800	2,800–3,200
	19–30	2,400	2,600–2,800	3,000
	31–50	2,200	2,400–2,600	2,800–3,000
	51+	2,000	2,200–2,400	2,400–2,800

[a] These levels are based on Estimated Energy Requirements (EER) from the Institute of Medicine Dietary Reference Intakes macronutrients report, 2002, calculated by gender, age, and activity level for reference-sized individuals. "Reference size," as determined by IOM, is based on median height and weight for ages up to age 18 years and median height and weight for that height to give a BMI of 21.5 for adult females and 22.5 for adult males.

[b] Sedentary means a lifestyle that includes only the light physical activity associated with typical day-to-day life.

[c] Moderately active means a lifestyle that includes physical activity equivalent to walking about 1.5 to 3 miles per day at 3 to 4 miles per hour, in addition to the light physical activity associated with typical day-to-day life.

[d] Active means a lifestyle that includes physical activity equivalent to walking more than 3 miles per day at 3 to 4 miles per hour, in addition to the light physical activity associated with typical day-to-day life.

[e] The calorie ranges shown are to accommodate needs of different ages within the group. For children and adolescents, more calories are needed at older ages. For adults, fewer calories are needed at older ages.

Throughout this cookbook, we emphasize fruits and vegetables, whole grains, lean meats, beans, and nuts. These foods will help you lose weight, especially if you substitute them for fats and starches, and limiting fat helps fight heart disease and some cancers. Eating more fruits and vegetables will also lower your chances of getting some types of cancer and other diseases such as diabetes. They also help to make sure your body gets the vitamins, minerals, and fiber it needs for good health.

The recipes in *Eat to Defeat Menopause* are calorie conscious and follow the dietary guidelines for Americans recommended by the United States Department of Health and Human Services, so that the percent of calories per recipe is as follows:

Total Fat 30%
Saturated Fat 7–10%
Carbohydrates 50–55%
Protein 15–18%

Occasionally, one of the recipes might contain a little more fat or calories. We know everyone likes a special treat! You'll know by the number of calories so you can combine it with a salad or have fewer calories or fat in your next meal, so your eating experience for the day will stay healthy.

The average woman at menopause eats too many calories and consumes too much salt and sugar. Notice in the table on the previous page that after age 30, women need fewer calories than when they were younger. The number of calories you need goes down even further after age 50. This book offers information and recipes to improve health at menopause and beyond. I have a large extended family, and we and my Italian friends know to eat small portions at a leisurely pace. In Italian households it is rare to be offered fattening appetizers before dinner, such as chips or cheesy crackers. An *antipasto* (an Italian appetizer) is usually served as the first course of the meal. It can be as simple as a slice of fresh melon with a thin slice of *prosciutto* (ham) or olives, or tuna and beans, or a variety of seafood. This type of eating will not lead to weight gain. And, whoever said we should stay away from pasta? Nonsense! Just eat pasta as the Italians do, not weighted down in heavy meat and cheese sauces. Pasta comes in a variety of shapes and sizes. You can add light sauces as well as fresh vegetables or seafood, all of which provide important nutrients and delicious taste.

To Italians, pasta is the staff of life. It contains complex carbohydrates, especially if the pasta is whole grain, and is a high-energy food. It is also, contrary to popular belief, low in calories. It's the sauce on the top that adds the calories, as well as the pounds. My roots are in Sicily, and we Sicilians eat very little meat. Instead, one of our favorite foods, especially in the Mediterranean and also in Sicilian households, is fish.

The fish markets in Sicily are their pulse of life. They are always stocked with a wide variety of fresh fish. Italians don't overcook their vegetables or serve them with butter. Instead, they are complemented with a few drops of olive oil, garlic, or other fresh herbs that tickle their palate. Salads are always served at the end of the meal following the main course and act as a natural aid to digestion. Salads are simply dressed with a light dressing of olive oil, red wine vinegar, and fresh herbs.

In the Jewish tradition, foods play a central role. Each holiday has its own special meals, and for certain holidays, such as Passover, the entire experience revolves around the Seder dinner. Some of the traditional Jewish foods have not always been as healthy as they could be. Recipes included chicken fat, lots of salt, and organ meats to create dishes such as chopped liver. Today much of that has changed. Chicken fat has been replaced with monounsaturated and polyunsaturated oils; the amount of salt has been reduced; and chopped liver is being made with vegetarian substitutes such as lentils, mushrooms, and walnuts. Bubbie is constantly updating ingredients to create healthy recipes.

So, now let's separate fact from fiction about our diet and what may help us to lose weight.

DIET FACTOIDS AND FICTIONOIDS

There are a lot of misconceptions about our diet. Here are a few:

Fictionoid: *Skipping meals will help me lose weight.*
Factoid: Skipping meals can make us ravenously hungry. That makes us more likely to snack or eat more calories when we eat next. If you do need to snack, grab a piece of fruit or 6 to 8 almonds or walnuts.

Fictionoid: *The best way to lose weight is to cut out starches (carbohydrates).*
Factoid: What we need to avoid are *simple* carbohydrates, such as refined sugar, concentrated sweeteners, honey, white flour, and alcohol. They are absorbed rapidly and make our body produce high levels of insulin that quickly lowers our blood sugar level, leaving us feeling hungry soon afterward. Insulin released like this also creates more fat on our body.

On the other hand, *complex* carbohydrates, such as fruits and vegetables, whole grains, and legumes, are absorbed slowly so insulin levels don't have to quickly rise, and our blood sugar level stays more constant. White flour is whole-wheat flour with the bran and fiber refined out of it. If you want pasta, just eat whole-wheat pasta or whole-wheat bread, or eat brown rice instead of refined rice and, voilà, you're eating complex carbohydrates.

Fictionoid: *I should cut out all fat from my diet.*
Factoid: The short answer is no, you shouldn't. You need at least 6% of the food you eat to be fat in order to make hormones and build cells, and for other important functions. But the average American diet is about 40% fat, and that increases your risk of heart disease. The recommended amount of fat by most US government agencies is 30%. According to Dr. Dean Ornish, from a weight-gain point of view, fat is fat whether it comes from healthy oils like olive oil or from ice cream—a tablespoon of any fat, including olive oil, has 14 grams of fat, which is about the same as a scoop of ice cream. So if you eat a lot of fat from either oil or ice cream, you will gain weight. From a health point of view, we should avoid *hydrogenated* or *trans fats* because they increase our risk of heart disease. Read the labels and limit these. Harvard researchers have shown that women who eat high levels of trans–fatty acids have a 50% greater risk of heart disease than those who eat the least. "Good" fats are called *monounsaturated* fats (found in olive oil, canola oil, olives, some nuts, and avocados) or *polyunsaturated* fats (found in fish, seafood, soybeans, and whole grain).

Fictionoid: *The only way to lose weight is to starve yourself.*
Factoid: Not so. It is important to eat smart. A diet of largely complex carbohydrates that includes fruits, vegetables, whole grains, and legumes with moderate amounts of non-fat dairy and egg whites will fill you up—and help you lose weight. If you exercise and burn extra calories, all the better. Stay away from breads, use portion control, and don't keep eating once you feel full.

Red Hot Tip #1   AVOID LIQUID CANDY

What happens to your weight when you eat too much candy? It goes up, right? That's because candy has a lot of sugar and almost no nutrients that your body needs to stay healthy and strong.

We call soda "liquid candy," and here is why. There are 12 to 15 heaping teaspoons of sugar in every 12-ounce can of soda. In the 1950s, Americans drank four times as much milk as soda. Today, the US Department of Agriculture says Americans drink almost four times as much soda as milk. How does this affect you?

In 2004, doctors studied 51,603 women.[3] First, they made sure everything was the same except how much soda people drank. Here is what they found. Women who increased the number of sugar-sweetened carbonated soft drinks from 1 or fewer sodas per week to 1 or more sodas per day gained a lot of weight. Those women who went from 1 or more sodas per day to 1 or fewer sodas per week lost a lot of weight. And those women who did not change the amount of soda they drank did not have a change in their weight. They found the same thing was true for sweetened fruit punch.

You might think that just drinking a diet soda would solve the problem. Maybe not. Another report[4] studied what happened when men and women were give sugar-sweetened soda, artificially sweetened soda, or no soda for 3 weeks. Both men and women gained a lot of weight if they drank the sugar-sweetened sodas. But only the men lost weight if they drank the artificially sweetened soda. Here is the tip: Want an easy way to lose weight? Stop drinking soda and other sweetened drinks and drink more water and non-fat milk.

UNDERSTANDING THE GLYCEMIC INDEX[5]

Did you know that carbohydrates are not all created equal? Some, such as a soda or a potato, can quickly raise your blood sugar. Others, such as fruits and vegetables (besides potatoes), don't raise your blood sugar level much at all. How quickly a carbohydrate increases your blood sugar level is given a value called the Glycemic Index, or GI. Foods are ranked from 0 to 100. Pure glucose has a value of 100. Choosing carbohydrates with medium or low GI can help you lose weight, reduce the risk of heart disease, control diabetes, reduce hunger feelings, and keep you fuller longer.

How does this happen? When your blood sugar rises quickly, it triggers a large release of the hormone insulin to bring your blood sugar level back down to normal. That quick lowering of your blood sugar causes you to feel hungry again in a few hours. Did this ever happen to you? If you said yes, it's time to change that. Over time, a high GI diet will increase your risk of diabetes, heart disease, and even cancer. Choosing carbohydrates with a medium or low GI keeps your blood sugar level more constant and lowers your risk of those diseases and obesity. That's why the recipes in this cookbook include their GI. You can find out more about GI at www.glycemicindex.com.

Low GI = 55 or less
Most fruits, vegetables (except potatoes and watermelon), grainy breads, milk, soymilk, soy, fish, eggs, meat, beans and peas, nuts, and brown rice have a low GI.

Medium GI = 56 to 69
Whole-wheat products, basmati rice, and sweet potatoes have a medium GI.

High GI = 70 or more
Many breakfast cereals, baked potatoes, white bread, instant white rice, and doughnuts have a high GI.

The Glycemic Load (GL) tells you how much of a carbohydrate is in a serving of a particular food. So if a food has a high GI, such as watermelon, but there isn't a lot of sugar in it, its GL is low. Here is a tip: If you choose to eat a high GI food, eat a smaller portion so the GL stays medium to low. Here are the values to look for:

High GL = 20 or more
Medium GL = 11 to 19
Low GL = 10 or less

I'M NOT HAVING A HOT FLASH. I'M HAVING A POWER SURGE.
—*Attributed to Alice Lotto Stamm*

Every 4 minutes another American woman enters menopause. The infamous "M" word. The Change. But it's OK. It's not the end. It's a new beginning. Women live one-third of their lives after menopause; and those same women who gave the world reproductive choice and the feminist movement want to know how to stay healthy, strong, and active forever. For many women, menopause, and the stage of life it represents, is very positive. You can't get pregnant, so there's more sexual freedom. And if the kids ever get a job and move out of the house, there is often more time and money to enjoy life. A Harris poll found that women who turn 50 today view themselves as younger than their parents did at that age, and 51% of 752 postmenopausal women surveyed by the North American Menopause Society reported that they were happier and more fulfilled than they were in their 20s, 30s, and 40s.

 To hear the song "Red Hot Mama," go to www.healthrockwomen.com/music.

UNDERSTANDING THE LINGO

The word *menopause* has nothing to do with getting old. *Menopause* comes from two Greek words for "monthly" and "cessation"—*pausis* (cessation) and the root *men* (month)—it just means you don't have periods anymore. That's usually because a woman's ovaries no longer make enough estrogen to have a menstrual cycle (*natural* or *spontaneous* menopause). But it can also happen either when a woman's ovaries are removed by surgery (*surgical* menopause), or destroyed by radiation treatments, chemotherapy, or some other drug (*induced* menopause). A woman has to wait a full year after her last period to be sure it's menopause and not just a very irregular period (unless her ovaries are removed—*oophorectomy*). *Postmenopause* refers to all the years after menopause. Having a hysterectomy (an operation to remove the uterus) stops menstruation, but it does not cause menopause unless the ovaries are also removed.

A hysterectomy is the most common major surgery performed in women in the United States—more that 600,000 each year. Hysterectomy, with or without removing the ovaries, causes more frequent and severe symptoms than natural menopause, and that can make it more difficult to function at home or at work. According to the North American Menopause Society, more than two-thirds of women in North America will have hot flashes. Having a hysterectomy and an oophorectomy seems to turn up the flame and make them hotter.

Even though women are living longer than ever before, the age of natural menopause hasn't changed much over the past few centuries—51.4 years. But any time between ages 40 and 55 is normal. It often happens around the same time as one's mother or sister. *Premature* menopause means it occurs before age 40, and that happens to about 1 to 2% of women. *Perimenopause* means "around menopause" and refers to the months and years (up to 10 or 12) leading up to menopause plus 1 year after menopause.

A NATURAL BRIDGE CROSSED OVER BY MANY

Baby boomers, those of us born from 1946 to 1964, are reaching 50, big time—about 6,000 per day in United States. The same people who wanted to change the world in the

1960s are themselves starting to change. Today, if a woman reaches 50 without getting heart disease or cancer, she can expect to live to be 92. Sixty is the new 50. Menopause is just the next phase in a long life, complete with its benefits and its challenges. Realizing that menopause is a natural and inevitable next phase of life is valuable. It allows a person to stop asking, "How do I stop aging?" and begin asking the question posed by a prominent yogi, Hari Kaur Khalsa,[6] "How do I remain graceful throughout life's challenges?"

WHAT IS MENOPAUSE AND PERIMENOPAUSE?

YESTERDAY IS ALREADY A DREAM
AND TOMORROW IS ONLY A VISION,
BUT TODAY, WELL LIVED,
MAKES EVERY YESTERDAY A DREAM OF HAPPINESS
AND EVERY TOMORROW A VISION OF HOPE.
—*Anonymous*

Ann Louise Gittleman begins her book *Before the Change* by saying, "Peri-what?" She goes on to ask the very question most other 40-plus-year-old women ask as they enter perimenopause and approach menopause, "What on earth is happening to my body?" Suddenly an active woman who is used to juggling her work while managing the household, carpooling the kids, and organizing the social calendar starts waking up at 4 AM with heart palpitations and feeling anxious and depressed.

After a while she becomes a little more exhausted, a little more irritable, and notices she has a shorter attention span and a shorter fuse. Throw in a few mood swings, headaches, and trouble remembering where the car is parked, and suddenly you've got a woman convinced she is having a heart attack or has a brain tumor or a psychiatric problem. Sound familiar?

Many of the perimenopausal women we talk with have been to a doctor, had a normal EKG, and then are prescribed an antidepressant or a sleeping tablet for what seems like anxiety, depression, or a sleep disturbance. Many times the woman doesn't realize that the root of her symptoms is, you guessed it, perimenopause.

HORMONES IN PERIMENOPAUSE AND MENOPAUSE

Ever ride a rollercoaster? Ups and downs, right? That's what your hormones are like during menopause. Estrogen and progesterone levels plunge and soar and stop working together with precision. Your hormones act as though you're going through puberty, only backwards. Remember how that felt? Wacky menstrual periods—often lighter but sometimes heavier, sometimes farther apart, or even skipped, but often closer together. And when all of those mood swings and other symptoms kick in, it can feel like a raging case of PMS. And in many ways it is.

Like puberty, different women have different experiences. And why not? People are different before perimenopause, why shouldn't they be different during it? Fortunately, most women don't experience all of the symptoms of perimenopause. The good news is, even though it is a challenge, perimenopause is only temporary.

COMMON SYMPTOMS OF PERIMENOPAUSE

- Hot flashes
- Insomnia
- Menses irregularities
- Memory problems (usually caused by disturbed sleep)
- Weight gain

- Vaginal dryness
- Heart palpitations
- Lower sexual desire
- Depression
- Anxiety
- Mood swings
- Bone loss

THERE IS MORE THAN ONE ESTROGEN

Your body makes three major estrogens. These are the ones everyone now calls *bioidentical* estrogens. Their names are estr*one* (E1), estra*diol* (E2), and estr*iol* (E3). Most of the estradiol is made in the ovaries. Some estrone is made in the ovaries, but it is mostly made in the body's fat cells. If you guess that women with more body fat make more estrone, you're right. More estrone is good news for some women because it may lower their symptoms of menopause. But women who are 25 to 50 pounds overweight have a 3 times higher risk of uterine cancer, and if they are more than 50 pounds overweight, they are 9 times as likely to get uterine cancer. Women who are too thin and who have too little fat on their body may stop having periods because their body does not produce enough estrogen. These are the very reasons it's important to control your weight and why we want you to eat healthy!

ANALYSIS OF A HOT FLASH

What actually happens during a hot flash? The heat turns up, your heart speeds up, blood flow to the skin increases, and your face turns red. You are an official Red Hot Mama! Sweating often follows, particularly on the upper body. When the sweat evaporates a few minutes later, the body cools down and you may feel chilled.

Ode to Soy and Hot Flashes

Drenched with sweat
I wake again
'Cause I'm afraid of estrogen
Can't recall how long it's been
Since I could sleep the night.

Trying soy could do no harm
It stopped the heat, though
I'm still warm.
Now I feel my life is charmed
'Cause I can sleep the night.

Experts say, "It's not the same
As Estrogen," they all complain.
But it sure helped turn down
the flame.
And I can sleep the night!
—Mache Seibel, MD[1]

Nobody knows for sure why they start. The thermostat that regulates your temperature is out of whack. Some tips to avoid them are listed below.

Will hot flashes happen to you? Most women will have at least some. Women who are too thin and who have lower blood estrogen levels are more likely to have hot flashes. And the lower the estrogen level, the more severe the hot flashes. The good news is that for most women, after 3 to 5 years they begin to taper off.

RED HOT TIPS TO HELP AVOID HOT FLASHES

Avoid personal triggers. Everybody has them and you'll know yours. Examples are a warm room or using a hair dryer, psychological stress, or a confining space.

Exercise regularly. It reduces stress and helps with sleep. Yoga, meditation, tai chi, or massage is particularly useful.

Stay cool. Dress in light nightclothes, layer your bedding so you can take it off easily at night, keep a frozen cold pack under the pillow and turn your pillow often so the surface feels cool.

Breathe deep and slow. When a hot flash begins, take slow, deep breaths through your nose and release out through your mouth. This is a great yoga technique.

LET YOUR FOOD BE YOUR MEDICINE, AND YOUR MEDICINE BE
YOUR FOOD.
—*Hippocrates*

HOT FLASHES AND INSOMNIA

One of the reasons we wrote this book is that what you eat
and drink can affect menopausal symptoms. We want all of you
Red Hot Mamas to eat to defeat menopause. Here are some
Red Hot Tips that may reduce hot flashes and help with sleep:

Say **NO** to:
Large meals. When you eat a large meal, the body's digestion
brings blood into the abdomen, raises body temperature, and
voilà, tells the hypothalamus part of the brain to send a signal
that causes hot flashes. Eating smaller meals can help reduce
the number of hot flashes.

Caffeine. Coffee, tea, colas, and even dark chocolate
contain caffeine. They may trigger hot flashes as well as affect
the quality of your sleep. So drink more water and avoid
caffeine, especially in the late afternoon and at night. Substitute
decaffeinated beverages, teas that are caffeine free, and water.
Too much caffeine can also take calcium out of your bones.

Alcohol. Alcohol can increase the number and intensity of
hot flashes and affect sleep, mood swings, and your weight.
Heavy alcohol use can even lead to osteoporosis because it
prevents bone cells from building new bone. Too much alcohol
also increases the chances of falling and breaking a bone. There
may be an even more important reason to limit alcohol. We've
been told for a decade that drinking a glass of red wine every
day may be good for your heart. But several recent studies
have found that drinking as little as one alcoholic beverage a
day can increase a woman's chances of getting breast cancer.
Play it safe—limit yourself to no more than one drink a day.

Here is another Red Hot Tip: If you are going to a cocktail party, always eat something solid *before* you get there so you won't go overboard on the appetizers.

Hot spicy foods. Cayenne, chili peppers, wasabe, and hot mustard can turn up the heat.

Say **YES** to:

Foods that contain phytoestrogens, which may help reduce hot flashes. These include soy foods such as edamame, tofu, and soy yogurt or milk, and even flaxseeds, sesame seeds, garlic, hummus, and veggie burgers are a few items to consider.

Carbohydrates and other sleep-promoting foods. Carbohydrate-rich foods may help if you are losing your snoozing time due to sleep issues. Studies suggest that eating carbs can increase the release of tryptophan, an amino acid that helps the brain manufacture the chemical serotonin, which helps people fall asleep. Try eating a piece of toasted whole-grain bread, or a small portion of another carbohydrate, before going to bed. Other foods that contain tryptophan are turkey, soy, cod, egg whites, or a glass of warm milk. Tryptophan helps promote sleep. Also, omega-3 fatty acids, which are found in fish such as salmon, trout, and tuna play a role in sleep induction. And don't forget cherries. They contain melatonin, which is a substance found in the body that helps regulate sleep.

HEADACHES

Headaches are a common problem during the menopause transition. They seem to increase at perimenopause, and hormone fluctuations may play a role in causing them. They also may be due to changes in our sleeping patterns. Daily supplementation with magnesium, riboflavin, and/or coenzyme Q10 is an effective and safe option for women who experience headaches.

Say **YES** to:
Foods that are rich in magnesium, such as almonds, black beans, broccoli (raw), halibut, okra, oysters, and scallops, among others.

Say **NO** to:
Alcohol (especially red wine), foods that contain monosodium glutamate (MSG), and cured meats such as salami and bologna.

BLOATING

During the menopause transition another common midlife symptom is bloating, which may be due to hormone fluctuations, an overproduction of estradiol, and the conversion of androgen (a so-called "male" hormone) to estrogen through a process called *aromatization,* which increases with age and body weight.

Say **YES** to:
Foods and herbs that have diuretic properties, such as celery seed, parsley, dandelion, juniper berries, asparagus, artichokes, melon, and watercress. And drink plenty of water and herbal teas.

Say **NO** to:
Sugary foods, salt and salty food products, and high-sodium foods such as frozen dinners and canned soups. Read the sugar and sodium content on food labels.

MOOD SWINGS

Many women during the menopause transition report symptoms of a decreased sense of well-being due to mood disturbances such as irritability and mood swings. Your food choices may be linked to some of these mood changes. When women eat better, they feel better. Good nutrition plays a major role in our moods. So it is important to understand which foods stabilize our moods and which ones to avoid.

Say **YES** to:
Omega-3 fatty acids foods such as tuna, salmon, and mackerel. Eat vegetables such as asparagus, Brussels sprouts, and beets, which are rich in B vitamins and folic acid. Green vegetables such as spinach and peas are high in folate, which may also help stabilize your mood because it's needed to make serotonin. Always use fresh vegetables whenever you can and don't forget that spinach can be used in salads as well. Chicken and turkey are also rich in vitamin B, which may also play a role in the production of serotonin in the body.

Say **NO** to:
Sugary foods, which cause a rise in your blood sugar and may increase mood disturbances.

SEX

Can food spice up your sex life? Recent information suggests that it can, though medical science is still scratching its head with skepticism. So let's take a look at some foods that *may* spice up your sex life.

Say **YES** to:
Granola, oatmeal, nuts, dairy, green vegetables, garlic, soybeans, and chickpeas. These foods contain L-arginine, which is thought to be helpful in improving sexual function.

Avocados contain potassium, which regulates thyroid hormones, and may enhance female libido. Eating chocolate helps release chemicals in your body that cause pleasure, similar to having sex.

Chocolate intake releases serotonin in the brain, producing feelings of pleasure. Chocolate also contains phenylalanine, which raises endorphins, making us feel good and less depressed. But sisters, indulge in moderation for its benefit, and try eating it as a prelude to lovemaking.

Asparagus is a vegetable to consider due to its richness in vitamin E. At nineteenth century weddings, asparagus was served because of its reputation as an aphrodisiac. Feast on fresh fruits such as strawberries, pomegranates, and grapes, which are rich in antioxidants and are not only sensual, they are also delicious. And eating chile peppers triggers the release of endorphins, those natural opioids that create a high that is like lovemaking. But remember, chile peppers can also trigger hot flashes.

Say **NO** to:
Alcohol, which affects blood flow and impacts testosterone levels and libido. It contributes to sexual dysfunction. Both women and men experience a reduction in sexual arousal and difficulty having orgasms, and men may have difficulty getting an erection.

CHANGES IN METABOLISM ARE THE NORM

Ever notice you can't eat as much as you used to without gaining weight? Metabolism first starts to slow down during your 30s, causing the percentage of lean muscle in your body to decrease while fat increases. During your 40s, things change even more. Your basal metabolic rate (BMR) drops by 4 to 5% each decade, making it even more important to eat healthy and to keep exercising. By the time you reach your 50s, your body needs 50 fewer calories each day than you did in your 40s in order not to gain weight. That is why it is so easy for pounds to sneak up on you if you waste your calories on poor food choices. Think healthy food choices! Think exercise! Think portion control!

In your 60s, most of any added weight will find its home in your abdominal area. Increasing girth increases your risk of high blood pressure, diabetes, and heart disease. By the seventh decade, it's common to lose muscle strength and tone and bone density. That's why we keep encouraging you to continue exercising, and if you can, to do weight training. And watch what and how much you eat. Burning off unwanted calories will help you fight off diseases and keep your muscles strong. It can also help keep your back straight so it doesn't hunch forward. See why this cookbook is making sense!

You know how they say as we get older we become more and more creatures of habit? It's true, even when it comes to food. A report in the *Journal of the American Medical Association* found that after a period of deliberate overfeeding, young men go back to eating less food, but elderly men continue to overfeed themselves. On the other hand, after a period of enforced underfeeding, young men increase their diet to make up for what they lost, but elderly men continue to underfeed themselves for up to 10 days.[7] So if an older person has to stay in the hospital or gets depressed and starts to eat less, we can't assume that they will quickly start eating again once the problem passes. It's important information, because between 30 and 50% of women 65 years and older are living alone, and are less likely to cook for themselves and more likely to either not eat or to go out and eat higher-caloric meals. These types of situations can cause eating habits to change and have a major effect on a person's nutrition.

Other factors also play a role. About a third of people over age 60 make less acid in their stomach, a condition called *hypochlorhydria*. These changes make it harder to absorb vitamins B6, B12, and D and riboflavin. In addition, our body makes vitamin D when our skin is exposed to sunshine. As we age, our skin changes and can't produce vitamin D as well as it once did, so we need even more vitamin D. Since we need vitamin D to absorb calcium, less calcium gets absorbed, and that's bad for our bones. On top of this, nearly 75% of women of all ages don't eat enough calcium to keep their bones strong. Use this cookbook to help solve these problems.

AM I TOO FAT (OR TOO THIN)

How do doctors determine if a person is under- or overweight? We use a tool called the *Body Mass Index* (BMI). It's a formula (weight in pounds ÷ height in inches^2 × 703) that uses your weight and your height together. Look down the first column to find your height and then scan across to your weight. Your BMI is the number on top of that column. A BMI in the low 20s is the goal. Below 18.5 is underweight. A BMI of 25 to 29.9 is considered overweight and 30 or more is obese.

Table 2. Body Mass Index (BMI)

	21	22	23	24	25	26	27	28	29	30
5'0"	107	112	118	123	128	133	138	143	148	153
5'1"	111	116	122	127	132	137	143	148	153	158
5'2"	115	120	126	131	136	142	147	153	158	164
5'3"	118	124	130	135	141	146	152	158	163	169
5'4"	122	128	134	140	145	151	157	163	169	174
5'5"	126	132	138	144	150	156	162	168	174	180
5'6"	130	136	142	148	155	161	167	173	179	186
5'7"	134	140	146	153	159	166	172	178	185	191
5'8"	138	144	151	158	164	171	177	184	190	197
5'9"	142	149	155	162	169	176	182	189	196	203
5'10"	146	153	160	167	174	181	188	195	202	207
5'11"	150	157	165	172	179	186	193	200	208	215

EXERCISE

When Karen was young (she wasn't always a Red Hot Mama), her mother used to tell her, "When I was your age, I had to walk 5 miles to go to school." Her mom was encouraging her to become more active and be less dependent on being driven everywhere. Her mom also used to say, "You'll understand when you're older." Well, she was right. Exercise is as important as eating healthy. Look at the benefits of exercise:

- Reduces risk of heart disease and osteoporosis
- Controls weight
- Improves appearance and self-esteem
- Improves sleep
- Decreases depression by raising endorphins

When you exercise, try to get your heart to beat at 60 to 75% of its maximum capacity. This will give you the best cardiovascular benefit without overtaxing your heart. The desired heart rate changes with your age and your health. Always discuss what is an ideal heart rate for you with your doctor. An advisable range is listed below.

Table 3. Target Heart Rate

Age	Beats per Minute
20	120–160
25	117–156
30	114–152
35	111–148
40	108–144
45	105–140
50	102–136
55	99–132
60	96–128
65	93–124
70	90–120

OSTEOPOROSIS (THINNING OF THE BONES)

If you are a Red Hot Mama, it's important that you bone up on how to prevent osteoporosis. Here is why: A healthy 50-year-old woman is just as likely to die of a complication of osteoporosis as she is to die of breast cancer. Many of you will get a mammogram. But have you gotten a bone density test?

According to the American College of Obstetricians and Gynecologists (ACOG), about 13 to 18% of American women age 50 or older have osteoporosis, and another 37 to 50% have osteopenia (mild bone loss that often leads to osteoporosis). Osteoporosis affects 28 million Americans, and 80% of them are women. The National Osteoporosis Foundation estimates that in 2010 that number will be 52 million. Every 20 seconds, another American breaks a bone because of osteoporosis. Nearly half of all women over 50 will break a bone because of osteoporosis. One in 4 men will too.

But there is no need to tiptoe around, afraid that calcium is silently oozing out of your bones, leaving you frail and vulnerable. Get a bone density test as menopause approaches. They have only 10% of the radiation received in a routine chest x-ray, and they diagnose the problem.

RED HOT TIPS AND HABITS YOU CAN CHANGE TO KEEP
BONES STRONG:

- If you smoke—quit!
- Exercise 30 minutes 3 to 5 times a week. Jogging, jumping rope, walking briskly, or lifting weights can increase bone density 3 to 5% a year.
- Limit alcohol to 1 glass of wine, 1 beer, or 1 ounce of spirits daily.
- Avoid high caffeine use.
- Limit salt and sodas; they increase calcium loss through your kidneys.
- Get 1,200 mg of calcium, 400 to 800 IU of vitamin D, and 400 mg of magnesium daily. If you don't get that much in your diet, take supplements.
- Eat healthy. Some of the recipes in this book can help lower your risk of osteoporosis and keep your bones strong.
- Check your vitamin D blood level. So many Red Hot Mamas have low levels and it's easy to fix with supplements. You can't absorb calcium without enough vitamin D.

HE THAT TAKES MEDICINE AND NEGLECTS DIET WASTES THE SKILLS OF THE PHYSICIAN.
~ *Chinese proverb*

Soy is one of the healthiest foods you can eat. It has lots of protein, minerals, vitamins, and a whole lot more. Soy contains *phyto*estrogens or "plant" estrogens—plant substances that act like weak estrogens in your body. If you're not eating soy, give it a try. There are so many ways to prepare it, so many ways to incorporate it into your daily diet, and so many ways to cook it, we're sure you can find a way to enjoy it. Especially when you realize it can reduce hot flashes and help prevent osteoporosis, heart disease, and maybe even some cancers.[1] Let's talk about soy.

SOYBEANS AND SOY FOODS MADE DIRECTLY FROM THEM

Soybeans
Soybeans come in several colors, depending on when they are harvested. The green ones that look like fuzzy Chinese snow peas are still slightly immature. They are called *edamame*. Later in the season, soybeans begin to dry and turn yellow, black, or brown. They look like black-eyed peas without the black eye.

Canned soybeans are ready to be used and can be added to chilis, stews, and soups right out of the can. Using the liquid in the can will save some of the B vitamins that might be lost from the canning process. Dried soybeans, like most other legumes, have to be soaked overnight to rehydrate them. It usually takes about 3 cups of water for each cup of soybeans. In the morning, drain off the water, cover them again with fresh water, simmer over low heat for 3 hours, and they are ready to be used in recipes. If you're using a tomato product in your recipe, it's better to add it when the dish is nearly done because tomatoes toughen the outer layer of the bean and take longer to soften. After they are cooked, eat them within the next few days.

Soy Flour

Soy flour is made by grinding up whole dried soybeans. It can't be used by itself, but it can replace up to 20% of the weight of all-purpose flour required in almost any recipe. You can also use soy flour as a substitute for eggs in recipes by adding 1 tablespoon of soy flour and 2 tablespoons of water for each egg called for.

Soy Powder

Soy powder is very similar to soy flour. The difference is that the soybeans are cooked before they are ground. It can be used to make soymilk, added as powdered milk to coffee, or added to recipes.

Soy Protein Isolates

Soy protein isolates is defatted soy flour with the fiber, carbohydrates, and moisture removed, but 90% of the protein left in. It is an excellent source of protein that adds texture to a variety of soy-based dairy foods, such as cheese, non-dairy frozen desserts, and coffee whiteners. It's also a major ingredient in soy hotdogs, soy ice cream, baby food, and meat analogues.

Textured Vegetable Protein (TVP)

Textured vegetable protein is a modern Western invention. Defatted soy flour is compressed until its protein fiber changes in structure. When water is added to it, the TVP gets very coarse, so it looks and feels like ground beef. Add a little chicken or beef flavoring and you've got a stew or the perfect taco or chili meat substitute. Adding up to 20% or less by weight to your next hamburger dish, it is the perfect hamburger extender; you can't taste the difference, but you will be getting 20% less animal fat from the same dish.

Soy Grits

Soy grits come from the whole bean, so they taste a lot like soybeans and retain 55 to 65% of the protein by weight and most of soy's beneficial contents. They are made by lightly toasting and hulling the soybeans, then either cracking or grinding them into small pieces. Because soy grits contain most of the fat, they become rancid if not refrigerated. You can use soy grits either as a breakfast cereal by stirring 1 part grits into 3 parts boiling water, then cover, lower the heat, and simmer until all the water is absorbed. It's not an instant breakfast, though. Unless the beans are presoaked, cooking takes about 45 minutes. Soy grits are a bit chewy, so they're a natural extender for hamburger or a great way to add texture to chili, stews, and spaghetti sauce.

Soy Sprouts

Soy sprouts are an excellent source of magnesium, folic acid, and vitamin C, and they are low in sodium. You can add them fresh to salads or cook them fast at low heat.

Okara

Okara is the pulp and hulls that remain after the soymilk is strained. Its name literally means "honorable hull." It is very high in fiber and protein. Okara is often described as having a coconut-like texture, which makes it a frequently used ingredient in granola bars, muffins, and cookies. It can also be found in vegetarian burgers. Keep your okara refrigerated and use it within a few days.

Soymilk and Products Made from Soymilk

Soymilk. Soymilk is an ancient drink, developed by the Chinese Buddhist monks who then brought it to Japan. Asians drink it daily the way we drink cow's milk in the United States. Soymilk was first available in the United States in the 1920s. Once the carton is opened, it must be refrigerated and used up within about a week.

Soymilk can be used for anything you use milk for, such as dry cereal and instead of milk to make cream of wheat or oatmeal. But you can also use it to make sauces, puddings, custards, or mousse. Soymilk is rich in iron, phosphorus, thiamine, copper, potassium, and magnesium, as well as vegetable protein.

Yuba. Yuba is the "skin" that forms on soymilk when it is heated. It isn't usually available in the United States, but it can be found widely in China and in gourmet shops in Japan, where it is considered a delicacy. Yuba is 52.4% protein and is commonly added to soups and stews. It can also be pressed into molds and made into imitation meat.

Soy Cheese. Soymilk can be made into cheeses just as cow's milk can. It is low in fat and cholesterol, and lactose free. If it is held together with calcium caseinate, that means it contains dairy. If isolated soy protein is used, it is dairy-free. Like soymilk, it comes as full-fat, low-fat or fat-free as mozzarella, jack, and Cheddar.

Soy Yogurt. Soy yogurt is a dairy-like product made by adding live bacteria cultures to soymilk. A 1-cup serving contains 12 grams of soy protein, no lactose, and no cholesterol. You can buy it plain or with fruit added, and as whole or low fat. Soy yogurt has a similar consistency to dairy yogurt so you can use it interchangeably for a snack or as an ingredient in foods such as sauces, milk shakes, and desserts.

Tofu. Tofu is also known as *bean curd* and *doufu*. It's inexpensive and easy to digest for young and old. Tofu is curdled soymilk. After the curdling agent is added to soymilk, it separates into curds and whey. Tofu is the soybean curds that are compressed into the white, spongy cubes seen in most health food stores and supermarkets. Tofu comes in several forms and all of them have to be kept refrigerated, except the dried variety. Keep any unused portion submerged in water and change the water daily.

Tofu acts as a flavor sponge—it soaks up the flavor of whatever it is cooked with. Crumble a block of firm tofu in your hand and add it to hamburger and it tastes like hamburger. Cut it into cubes and add it to soup or stir-fry it with your favorite seasonings and vegetables. The softer forms of tofu are also sweeter and make a great choice for combining with your favorite fruits and whipping up in the blender. They also make great puddings and cream pies because they take up the taste of the chocolate or whatever flavor you add.

FERMENTED FORMS OF SOY

Tempeh

Tempeh (pronounced TEM-pay) is made from whole soybeans cooked with a mold, *Rhizopus,* from the hibiscus plant, at a warm temperature for 18 to 24 hours. The tempeh emerges as a chunky bean cake covered with an edible white mold.

Tempeh has a strong, distinctive taste with a chewy consistency that makes it a great meat substitute. You can marinade it and barbecue or grill it, steam it, or prepare it as you would tuna fish by grating it up and mixing it with mayonnaise, celery, and onions. A 3-ounce serving has about 150 calories, 16 grams of protein, and 6 grams of fiber. It you notice small gray or black flecks in your tempeh, it just means that it is naturally fermented. You can refrigerate it for up to a week or freeze it for up to several months.

Natto

Natto is another fermented soy food made from cooked whole soybeans. It is made by mixing in a bacteria culture with the soybeans and allowing them to ferment in plastic bags. In Japan it is used as a spread, at breakfast or dinnertime, or with *shoyu* (traditional soy sauce) and mustard. Natto is high in protein and rich in fiber, but lower in sodium than either miso or soy sauce. It's also a good source of iron, minerals, and B vitamins. If you are taking a class of antidepressants called MAO inhibitors, be careful eating natto. It contains the amino acid tyramine, which can dangerously elevate your blood pressure.

Miso

Miso is made with soybeans alone or soybeans combined with a grain such as barley or rice together with salt and a mold culture and left for up to 3 years in a cedar vat to ferment. It comes in a smooth and a chunky variety. A tablespoon of miso has 680 milligrams of sodium compared with table salt, which has 6,589 milligrams of sodium. Miso is a great source of protein (12–21%), comparable to eggs (13%), or even chicken (20%). Like natto, it contains the amino acid tyramine that can increase your blood pressure if you are taking a class of antidepressants known as MAO inhibitors.

Soy Sauce

Everyone who has gone out for Chinese food sees soy sauce either on the table or in the packet you come home with. The soy sauce we know in America is different from the traditional soy sauce in Asia that is known as *shoyu*. Shoyu is made by adding a mold to cooked soybeans and a grain, then fermenting them in salty brine for 1 to 1½ years. The soy sauces we're used to buying in bottles at the supermarket are really defatted soybean meal and wheat mixed with chemicals, corn syrup, and food coloring. Shoyu is sometimes called *tamari,* but that name is also used for the liquid that is left over when miso is made.

FLAXSEED

Flaxseed is another food that has been eaten for thousands of years. Flaxseeds are still popular in Asia, Scandinavia, and Africa. They look a lot like sesame seeds, except they are dark brown and have a pleasant nutty taste. In ancient times they were known as linseed, and the plant's fibers were woven into cloth, paper, and rope. In fact, the Egyptians used this type of cloth for wrapping mummies.

Flaxseeds contain about 18% protein and they are a rich source of calcium, potassium, and B vitamins. They are also a source of boron, a micronutrient considered important in conditions like arthritis and that may enhance levels of the body's own estrogen.

Flaxseeds are a rich source of the phytoestrogens known as *lignans*. Many women say that flaxseed helps reduce their hot flashes, but there is still only a small amount of scientific data to support their reports. If you do want to use flaxseeds to help with hot flashes, try eating 1 to 2 tablespoons of flaxseed oil daily, grinding up flaxseeds and spreading them on your salad, or adding them to your cereal, or consider some of the new Flax & Soy products made into cereals and bars.

Flaxseeds are also high in soluble fiber. In fact, soaking them overnight in water turns the flaxseeds into a gelatinous mass that makes a gentle fiber and a great cooking ingredient. You can also grind up the seeds to make flaxseed cereals, crusts, and snack bars. Flaxseeds can also be found as powders that are more a laxative than a cooking ingredient, and flax oil, which usually does not have many lignans because they stay behind with the residue of the seeds. Flax oil is a good source of omega-3 fatty acids. Be sure to buy only fresh, refrigerated flax oil in opaque bottles that have an expiration date. When it's fresh it has a nutty taste. When it's old it tastes bitter and even

a bit like fish oil. When that happens, throw it out and buy a
new bottle.

OMEGA-3 FATTY ACIDS (FISH OIL)

Did your mother ever give you cod liver oil? Once again, mother
knew best! Fish oil contains a lot of omega-3 fatty acids. Studies
show omega-3s are a type of fat that lowers your risk of heart
disease and helps to lower cholesterol, and they are good for your
joints and your brain. Omega-3s may even help your skin look good.

How much do you need? Eating fish twice a week or taking
a daily supplement containing 800 to 1,000 milligrams
(0.8–1 gram) should be about right. Because fish does contain
mercury, which can be bad for you, if you want to eat more fish
or take higher doses of supplements, talk with your doctor. Our
cookbook has included a number of great recipes that contain
fish and seafood as a delicious way to get your omega-3s.

Here are some examples of how to get 1.5 grams of omega-3s
by eating different types of fish:[8]

Anchovies, herring, mackerel, salmon: 1 serving (3 ounces)
Albacore tuna, sablefish, sardines: 1¼ servings (3.75 ounces)
Blue fin tuna, trout: 1½ servings (4.5 ounces)
Halibut, swordfish: 2 servings (6 ounces)
Fresh water bass, oysters: 2½ servings (7.5 ounces)
Sea bass: 3 servings (9 ounces)
Shrimp, pollack: 3½ servings (10.5 ounces)

EAT YOUR VEGGIES!

Do you remember Popeye holding a can of spinach? He knew that green leafy vegetables are good for you. Spinach has only 30 calories per cup and is a great source of calcium, potassium, and vitamins, and it helps protect us from diseases such as osteoporosis, heart disease, and colon cancer. An article in July 2009 in the British journal *Cancer* found that vegetarians are 12% less likely to develop cancer than meat eaters, and 45% less likely to develop certain cancers, such as cancers of the blood, stomach, and bladder. That's because vegetables have antioxidants, substances that prevent pieces of molecules from connecting together to form cancer-causing chemicals. In general, fresh spinach contains a lot more vitamins than the canned stuff Popeye ate.

You don't have to wait until dinner to have vegetables. You can put spinach or sautéed asparagus in an egg white omelet or in a salad, or you can add it to a pot of soup. Try to stay away from creamed vegetables. They may taste good, but the extra calories will lead to unwanted weight and the cream isn't heart healthy. One cup of cooked kale has more calcium than a cup of milk. Other calcium-rich vegetables include collard greens, chard, broccoli, and dandelion leaves, to name a few. Steaming is an excellent way to cook vegetables because it prevents loss of vitamins and minerals in cooking and it's fast and easy to do. And keep your refrigerator stocked with other vegetables that are healthy and crunchy and can be eaten raw. Instead of going for the M&M's, reach for radishes, carrots, cucumbers, broccoli, bell peppers, blanched green beans or snow peas, cherry tomatoes, or soy nuts, all of which will satisfy that craving for something crunchy many of us get, particularly before the dinner hour. Make a healthy salad with roasted vegetables, black olives, beans, and a healthy protein such as tuna or tofu. Choose a wide variety of salad greens, including arugula, spinach, watercress, and more. Don't be afraid of a squash!

UNDERSTANDING CHOLESTEROL

Cholesterol is a waxy, fat-like substance that is part of every cell in our body—our brain, nerves, muscles, skin, liver, intestines, and heart. Our body also uses cholesterol to make vitamin D and many hormones, including estrogen. But when our body has too much cholesterol, it can end up lining our blood vessels, making them narrower and hard and increasing our risk of heart disease. And heart disease is the number one cause of death for women in menopause. So the recipes in this cookbook focus on keeping your cholesterol levels down.

In addition to cholesterol, there are several other kinds of fats in our blood. Since high blood cholesterol increases your risk of having a heart attack, it's important to check your cholesterol levels regularly and know what the results mean. Here is some general information to help you understand "the numbers."

Red Hot Tip #3   WHAT DO MY CHOLESTEROL LEVELS MEAN?[9]

TOTAL BLOOD CHOLESTEROL
Desirable Level: Less than 200 mg/dL (milligrams per deciliter of blood)
Borderline High: 200 to 239 mg/dL
High Risk: 240 mg/dL and higher

HDL ("good") CHOLESTEROL
HDL stands for high-density lipoprotein. HDL is considered the "good" cholesterol because it protects you from having a heart attack. It's different from the other cholesterol levels; the higher your HDL, the better.

Several things can help you increase your HDL level: Quit smoking, lose excess weight, eat a good diet (see why we're doing this cookbook?), and exercise. It's simple—healthy lifestyle changes can increase your HDL and decrease your risk of heart attack.

	For Men	For Women
Desirable Level:	45 mg/dL or higher	55 mg/dL or higher
At Risk:	Less than 35 mg/dL	Less than 45 mg/dL

LDL ("bad") CHOLESTEROL

LDL stands for low-density lipoprotein. It's part fat and part protein. LDL is made in the liver and travels in the blood to the tissues of the body. A high level of LDL means there is a higher risk of heart disease. If you already have heart or vascular disease or diabetes, many doctors want your LDL level to be less than 100 mg/dL, or even less than 70 mg/dL.

Desirable Level:	Less than 130 mg/dL
Borderline:	130 to 159 mg/dL
High:	160 mg/dL or higher

What should my TRIGLYCERIDE level be?

Being overweight, drinking a lot of alcohol, and eating refined carbohydrates and saturated fats can increase your triglyceride level. Diabetes and some other medical problems can also increase your triglyceride level, which can put you at risk of coronary artery disease, low HDL levels, high blood pressure, and diabetes.

Normal:	Less than 150 mg/dL
High:	150 to 400 mg/dL
Very High:	Greater than 400 mg/dL

Red Hot Tip #4   UNDERSTANDING MYPYRAMID.GOV: STEPS TO A HEALTHIER YOU[10]

Every five years, the Departments of Agriculture (USDA) and Health and Human Services (HHS) join forces to write new dietary guidelines. The last guide was published in 2005. Another comes out late in 2010. Here are the key points you need to know:

1. Grains: Wheat, rice, oats, cornmeal, barley, and other cereals are grains. Make half your grains whole and avoid refined grains because they remove the bran and germ portions of the grain kernel, which also removes the fiber. If you do eat refined grains, make sure they are *enriched,* meaning the makers put back in the B vitamins and iron that are removed during the refining process. The fiber in whole grains helps you eat more slowly and fill up naturally, and this helps prevent overeating.

   a. Eat at least 3 ounces of whole-grain bread, cereal, crackers, rice, or pasta every day.

   b. Look for "whole" before the grain name on the list of ingredients.

2. Vegetables: Do you remember when your mother used to say, "Eat your vegetables, they're good, and they're good for you"? She was right! To stay well, eat a lot of them; more as you grow older. Because needs change with age, we've added a chart from the Centers for Disease Control (CDC) to make it clear. If you're physically active, you may be able to eat even more and not gain weight. Eating vegetables daily helps prevent certain diseases, including some cancers, and helps control your weight. According to a study published in May 2009,[11] only 29.4% of Americans eat 3 to 5 servings of vegetables per day, and only 16.4% eat 2 to 4 servings of fruit per day. Eat your vegetables. They're good, and they're good for you.

Table 4. Recommended Daily Amount for Vegetables

	Age	Daily Recommendation
Children	2–3 years old	1 cup
	4–8 years old	1½ cups
Girls	9–13 years old	2 cups
	14–18 years old	2½ cups
Boys	9–13 years old	2½ cups
	14–18 years old	3 cups
Women	10–30 years old	2½ cups
	31–50 years old	2½ cups
	51+ years old	2 cups
Men	19–30 years old	3 cups
	31–50 years old	3 cups
	51+ years old	2½ cups

How much is a cup?[12] According to the CDC, 1 cup of raw or cooked vegetables or vegetable juice, or 2 cups of raw leafy greens is equal to 1 cup from the vegetable group. Here is a chart that makes it clear:

Table 5. How Much Is a Cup of Vegetables?

	Amount that counts as 1 cup of vegetables	Amount that counts as ½ cup of vegetables
Dark-Green Vegetables		
Broccoli	1 cup chopped or florets 3 spears 5" long raw or cooked	
Greens (collards, mustard greens, turnip greens, kale)	1 cup cooked	
Spinach	1 cup, cooked 2 cups raw = 1 cup vegetables	1 cup raw
Orange Vegetables		
Carrots	1 cup, strips, slices, or chopped, raw or cooked 2 medium 1 cup baby carrots (about 12)	1 medium carrot About 6 baby carrots
Pumpkin	1 cup mashed, cooked	
Sweet potato	1 large baked (≥ 2¼" diameter) 1 cup sliced or mashed, cooked	
Winter squash (acorn, butternut, Hubbard)	1 cup cubed, cooked	
Dried Beans and Peas		
Dried beans and peas (such as black, kidney, pinto, or soybeans, or chickpeas, black-eyed peas, or split peas)	1 cup whole or mashed, cooked	
Tofu	1 cup ½" cubes (about 8 ounces)	1 piece 2½" × 2¾" × 1" (about 4 ounces)

	Amount that counts as 1 cup of vegetables	Amount that counts as ½ cup of vegetables
Starchy Vegetables		
Corn, yellow or white	1 cup 1 large ear (8–9" long)	1 small ear (about 6" long)
Green peas	1 cup	
White potatoes	1 cup diced, mashed 1 medium, boiled or baked 2½–3" diameter) French fried, 20 medium to long strips (2½–4" long)	
Other Vegetables		
Bean sprouts	1 cup cooked	
Cabbage, green	1 cup, chopped or shredded, raw or cooked	
Cauliflower	1 cup pieces or florets, raw or cooked	
Celery	1 cup, diced or sliced, raw or cooked 2 large ribs (11–12" long)	1 large rib (11–12" long)
Cucumbers	1 cup raw, sliced or chopped	
Green or wax beans	1 cup cooked	
Green or red bell peppers	1 cup chopped, raw or cooked 1 large pepper (3" diameter, 3¾" long)	1 small pepper
Lettuce, iceberg or head	2 cups raw, shredded or chopped	1 cup raw, shredded or chopped
Mushrooms	1 cup raw or cooked	
Onions	1 cup chopped, raw or cooked	
Tomatoes	1 large raw whole (3" diameter) 1 cup chopped or sliced, raw, canned, or cooked	1 small raw whole (1¼" diameter) 1 medium canned
Tomato or mixed vegetable juice	1 cup	½ cup
Summer squash or zucchini	1 cup cooked, sliced or diced	

3. Fruits:[13] Fruits are really good for you. They are a great source of vitamins, minerals, and fiber. Eat fruit as snacks and desserts. It doesn't matter if they are fresh, canned, frozen, or dried and may be whole, cut up, or puréed. But remember to buy dried fruits that are processed without sugar. The whole fruit has much fewer calories than the fruit juice. Unlike vegetables, 1 cup of fruit or 100% fruit juice, or ½ cup of dried fruit is equal to 1 cup of fruit.

Table 6. How Much Is a Cup of Fruit?

	Amount that counts as 1 cup of fruit	Amount that counts as ½ cup of fruit
Apple	½ large (3¼" diameter) 1 small (2½" diameter) 1 cup sliced or chopped, raw or cooked	½ cup sliced or chopped, raw or cooked
Applesauce	1 cup	1 (4-ounce) snack container
Banana	1 cup sliced 1 large (8–9" long)	1 small (less than 6" long)
Cantaloupe	1 cup diced or melon balls	1 medium wedge (1/8 of a medium melon
Grapes	1 cup whole or cut up 32 seedless grapes	16 seedless grapes
Grapefruit	1 medium (4" diameter) 1 cup sections	½ medium (4" diameter)
Mixed fruit (fruit cocktail)	1 cup diced or sliced, raw or canned, drained	1 (4-ounce) snack container, drained = 3/8 cup
Orange	1 large (3" diameter) 1 cup sections	1 small (2½" diameter)
Orange, mandarin	1 cup canned, drained	

	Amount that counts as 1 cup of fruit	Amount that counts as ½ cup of fruit
Peach	1 large (2¾" diameter) 1 cup sliced or diced, raw, cooked, or canned, drained 2 halves, canned	1 small (2" diameter) 1 (4-ounce) snack container, drained = 3/8 cup
Pear	1 medium pear (2½ per lb.) 1 cup sliced or diced, raw, cooked, or canned, drained	1 (4-ounce) snack container, drained = 3/8 cup
Pineapple	1 cup chunks, sliced or crushed, raw, cooked or canned, drained	1 (4-ounce) snack container, drained = 3/8 cup
Plum	1 cup sliced, raw or cooked 3 medium or 2 large plums	1 large plum
Strawberries	About 8 large berries 1 cup whole, halved, or sliced, fresh or frozen	½ cup whole, halved, or sliced
Watermelon	1 small wedge (1" thick) 1 cup diced or balls	6 melon balls
Dried fruit (raisins, prunes, apricots, etc.)	½ cup dried fruit	¼ cup dried fruit (1.5-ounce box raisins)
100% fruit juice (orange, apple, grape, grapefruit, etc.)	1 cup	½ cup

4. Milk: Milk and foods made from milk are part of this food group. Foods such as cream cheese, cream, and butter lose the calcium from the milk, so they are not in this group. Good examples are milk, yogurt, and cheese. Products that are low fat or fat-free are best because you get the calcium but save a lot of the calories. Sweetened milk products have sugar added, so it adds extra calories to your diet. If you are lactose intolerant, many lactose-intolerant people can still eat hard cheeses and yogurt. Soymilk is another great lactose-free choice and can be used as a milk substitute. Soy comes in light versions that have even fewer calories. You can also buy lactose-free cow's milk or use pills that have the lactase enzyme, so you can drink milk and milk products without side effects.

5. Meat and Beans: This part of the pyramid includes meat, poultry, fish, dried beans, eggs, and nuts.

Table 7. Color Chart of Food: Eat a Rainbow to Get Maximum Benefit[6]

Color	Food	Potential Benefit
Red	Tomatoes (rich, red color from lycopene)	Prevent prostate cancer and cancers of the bladder, pancreas, and digestive tract
	Peppers (hot and sweet)	Beta-carotene, vitamins C and A
	Beets	Fiber, which helps reduce risk of heart disease and some cancers; folic acid; and vitamin C
Orange	Winter squash, carrots, sweet potatoes	Beta-carotene, antioxidants
Green	Spinach Artichoke Broccoli, kale, collard greens, mustard greens Leafy vegetables	Iron Vitamin C and fiber Calcium Vitamin A, folic acid
Yellow	Summer squash Yellow pepper	Contains lutein, which may help prevent macular degeneration Vitamin C
Purple	Red cabbage	High in antioxidants, rich in vitamins, high in fiber; contain indoles, which are nitrogen compounds that may help protect against breast cancer
	Eggplant	Rich in nutrients, low in fat
White	Potatoes Parsnips Cauliflower	Complex carbohydrates, vitamins C and B6 High in fiber and folic acid Vitamin C and folic acid

Red Hot Tip #5   STEAM VEGGIES OR EAT THEM RAW

1. Use fruits and/or vegetables to replace some of the other foods you're eating to unleash their power and reduce calories in your diet.
2. Let off some steam! Steamed vegetables are delicious and low in calories. Steam until the color is bright and try not to overcook them.
3. Use low-fat or low-calorie dressings to add flavor.
4. Breading and frying or high-fat dressings or sauces add calories and fat to your diet.
5. If you boil vegetables, cut them into smaller pieces, ½ inch or smaller, to release their flavor quicker, within 20 minutes.

Red Hot Tip #6   SUBSTITUTIONS TO LOSE OR CONTROL WEIGHT

1. *Sour cream.* Replace with low- or non-fat sour cream or non-fat yogurt in dressings and sauces.
2. *Whole eggs.* Replace with liquid eggs or egg whites or a tablespoon of soy flour combined with 2 tablespoons of water.
3. *For breakfast.* Replace one of the eggs or half of the cheese in your omelette with spinach, onions, or mushrooms, or reduce the amount of cereal in your bowel and replace it with cut-up bananas, peaches, blueberries, or strawberries. Both add volume and flavor with fewer calories.
4. *For lunch.* Replace 2 ounces of the cheese and 2 ounces of the meat in your sandwich, wrap, or burrito with lettuce, tomatoes, cucumbers, or onions; replace 1 cup of noodles or 2 ounces of meat in your favorite broth-based soup with a cup of chopped vegetables, such as broccoli, carrots, beans, or red peppers.

5. *For dinner.* Replace 1 cup of the rice or pasta in your dish with 1 cup of chopped vegetables, such as tomatoes, squash, onions, peppers, or broccoli.
6. *Replace mayonnaise* on potato salad and sandwiches with fat-free mayonnaise or yogurt.
7. *Use non-fat sour cream or skim milk* thickened with cornstarch instead of cream in pasta sauces.

Red Hot Tip #7   BENEFITS OF SELECTED VEGETABLES[14]

Nutrient	Benefit	Vegetable Sources
Fiber	Decreases risk of heart disease; regulates bowels	Navy beans, kidney beans, black beans, pinto beans, lima beans, white beans, soybeans, split peas, chickpeas, black-eyed peas, lentils, artichokes
Folate	Reduces risk of having a baby with a brain or spinal cord injury; reduces homocysteine levels, which can lower risk of blood clots; may reduce risk of colon polyps	Black-eyed peas, cooked spinach, great northern beans, asparagus
Potassium	Helps maintain healthy blood pressure	Sweet potatoes, tomato paste, tomato purée, beet greens, white potatoes, white beans, lima beans, cooked greens, carrot juice, prune juice
Vitamin A	Keeps eyes and skin healthy; helps protect against infections	Sweet potatoes, pumpkin, carrots, spinach, turnip greens, mustard greens, kale, collard greens, winter squash, cantaloupe, red peppers, Chinese cabbage
Vitamin C	Helps heal cuts and wounds and keeps teeth and gums healthy	Red and green peppers, kiwi, strawberries, sweet potatoes, kale, cantaloupe, broccoli, pineapple, Brussels sprouts, oranges, mangoes, tomato juice, cauliflower

CALCIUM, CALORIE, AND FAT CONTENT OF COMMON DAIRY FOODS[1]   **Red Hot Tip #8**

	CALCIUM (mg)	CALORIES	FAT (g)
Milk and Milk Beverages			
Milk, whole, 1 cup	291	150	8
Milk, low-fat (2%), 1 cup	297	120	5
Milk, low-fat (1%), 1 cup	300	100	1
Milk, skim, 1 cup	302	85	0
Chocolate milk (1%), 1 cup	287	160	1
Buttermilk, 1 cup	285	100	2
Cheeses			
American, 1 oz.	174	105	9
Cheddar, 1 oz.	204	115	9
Cottage, low-fat (1%), 1 cup	155	160	2
Mozzarella, part-skim, 1 oz.	207	80	5
Swiss, 1 oz.	272	105	8
Yogurt			
Plain, low-fat, 8 oz.	415	145	3
Plain, non-fat, 8 oz.	452	125	0
Fruit, low-fat, 8 oz.	345	230	3
Coffee or vanilla, 8 oz.	389	194	3
Desserts			
Ice milk, hardened, 1 cup	176	185	6
Ice milk, soft serve, 1 cup	274	225	5
Ice cream (11% milk fat), I cup	176	270	14
Sherbet (2% fat), 1 cup	103	270	6

OTHER GOOD SOURCES OF CALCIUM

	CALCIUM (mg)	CALORIES	FAT (g)
Almonds	75	165	16
Broccoli, cooked, ½ cup	47	25	0
Collard greens, cooked, ½ cup	179	30	0
Kale, cooked, ½ cup	90	20	0
Salmon, pink, canned, with liquid and bones, 3 oz.	167	120	5
Sardines, canned in oil, with liquid and bones, 3 oz.	371	175	9
Snap beans, cooked, ½ cup	31	18	0
Tofu, firm, raw, ¼ block	166	118	7.1
Curdled with calcium salt	553	118	7.1
Tofu, regular, raw, ¼ block	122	88	5.6
Curdled with calcium salt	406	88	5.6
Soybeans, dry roasted, ½ cup	232	387	18.6
Soybeans, boiled, ½ cup	88	149	7.7
Soy protein concentrate, 1 oz.	102	93	0.13

Red Hot Tip #9   SMART SNACKS[15]

When you get hungry during the day, instead of reaching for a candy bar or bag of cookies or chips, think fruits and vegetables. Here are some great choices recommended by the CDC that are about 100 calories or less and perfect for a Red Hot Mama snack:

- a medium-sized apple (72 calories)
- a medium-sized banana (105 calories)
- 1 cup steamed green beans (44 calories)
- 1 cup blueberries (83 calories)
- 1 cup grapes (100 calories)
- 1 cup carrots (45 calories), broccoli (30 calories), or bell peppers (30 calories) with 2 tablespoons hummus (46 calories)

SIX RED HOT TIPS TO SIZE UP YOUR PORTION[16]

1. Three ounces of meat is about the size and thickness of a deck of cards
2. A medium apple or peach is the size of a tennis ball
3. One ounce of cheese is the size of 4 dice
4. A cup of broccoli is about the size of your fist
5. One teaspoon of butter or peanut butter is the size of the tip of your thumb
6. One ounce of nuts equals one handful

RED HOT TIPS WE'VE LEARNED FROM YOGIS[6]

- *Eat mindfully.* Eat slowly and experience your food; don't eat while watching TV and don't jump up immediately from the table when finished eating; relax a moment and digest.
- *Chew your food.* Digestion starts in your mouth and the more you chew your food the easier it will be to digest it. The yogis say, "There are no teeth in your stomach."
- *Listen to your body.* When you start to feel full, stop eating.
- *The "two-fist rule."* Make two fists with your hands and hold them in front of your stomach. This is the *total* amount of food you should have in your stomach at any one time. The yogic prescription for filling your stomach is one-third food, one-third water, and one-third space for digestion.
- *When to eat.* Eat your largest meal between 11 AM and 2 PM. Steamed vegetables or light vegetable salads are great choices for an evening meal. This helps prevent heartburn and acid reflux.
- *Eat a healthy snack.* Such as raisins and a few nuts or a banana in the late afternoon to keep your energy up and prevent overeating at dinner.

Red Hot Tip #10   RECOMMENDED DAILY CALCIUM INTAKE

- 4- to 8-year-olds   1,000 mg/day
- 9- to 18-year-olds   1,550 mg/day
- Pregnancy/breast-feeding   1,200 mg/day
- Premenopausal adult   1,000 mg/day
- Postmenopausal:
    Taking estrogen   1,000 mg/day
    Not taking estrogen   1,500 mg/day

Red Hot Tip #11   UNDERSTANDING FOOD LABELS

Food and Drug Administration (FDA) Guidelines for Common Food Claims:

Low Calorie: < 40 calories per serving
Low Cholesterol: < 20 mg of cholesterol and ≤ 2 g of saturated fat per serving
Reduced: 25% less of the specified nutrient or calories than the usual product
Good source of: provides at least 10% of the daily value of a particular vitamin or nutrient per serving
Calorie free: Less than 5 calories per serving
Fat free/sugar free: < ½ g of fat or sugar per serving
Low Sodium: < 140 mg of sodium per serving
High in: provides at least 20% of the daily value of a specified nutrient per serving
High fiber: 5 or more grams of fiber per serving

PLANT FOODS RICH IN PHYTOESTROGENS

The word *phyto* means "plant." These so-called plant or *dietary estrogens* have a chemical structure similar to estrogen, so they work in the body like a weak estrogen. The major phytoestrogen groups are isoflavones (found mostly in soy), flavones, coumestans, and lignans (found mostly in flaxseeds). Here are some other foods that have phytoestrogens:

Hummus	Dried dates, apricots, and prunes
Sesame seeds	Winter squash
Multigrain bread	Black beans
Alfalfa sprouts	Yams
Garlic	Walnuts, chestnuts, and pistachios
Mung bean sprouts	

MENOPAUSE MOMENTS: FOODS TO AVOID—AND FOODS THAT MAY HELP

Hot flashes. Avoid spicy foods, large meals, hot beverages, and alcohol. Add soy foods (edamame, tofu, soy nuts) to your diet.

Mood swings. Avoid sugar blasts such as donuts, sweetened soda, and candy. They send your blood sugar up and down quickly and bring your mood with it. Foods rich in B vitamins, such as beets, Brussels sprouts, and asparagus, may help relieve depression.

Headaches. Stay away from alcohol, MSG (monosodium glutamate—often in Chinese foods) and start eating magnesium-rich foods such as almonds and black beans.

Achy joints. Stay away from caffeinated drinks that rob your body of calcium and eat foods rich in omega-3 fatty acids such as salmon, which may reduce those aches and pains.

Memory lapses. Skipping meals can affect your memory and concentration. Remember when your mom said, "You can't start your day on an empty stomach"? She was right again. Antioxidant-rich foods such as blueberries and vegetables help slow down those memory lapses.

RED HOT TIPS FROM DEAN ORNISH TO HELP HIGH-FAT RECIPES LOSE SOME FAT[17]

- Use non-fat sour cream or non-fat yogurt instead of sour cream for dressings and sauces. Avoid boiling after adding non-fat yogurt to prevent it from separating.
- Use liquid egg substitute with no added fat or egg whites instead of whole eggs for baking.
- Use fat-free vegetable broth, wine, or water instead of oil for sautéing onions and garlic, and simmer vegetables until tender.
- Use fat-free Italian dressing as a substitute for oil-and-vinegar dressing, or drizzle salads and vegetables with balsamic vinegar, raspberry vinegar, or tarragon vinegar.
- Use non-fat mayonnaise or yogurt instead of mayonnaise on sandwiches and in potato salad. Whole-grain mustard alone is a great addition for flavor.
- Use prune purée or unsweetened applesauce instead of fat in baked goods. The purée is easy to make by whipping 4 ounces of pitted prunes and 5 tablespoons of water, or you can buy prepared fruit or prune purée, or use baby food. The ratio of prune purée to fat is .5:1. So, for ½ cup of butter, use ¼ cup of prune purée.

- Use non-fat sour cream or skim milk thickened with cornstarch instead of cream in pasta sauces. First dissolve cornstarch in a little cold water, then use 1 tablespoon of cornstarch for each 1 cup of liquid you are replacing. You can also use 1 tablespoon of flour whisked into 1 cup of non-fat milk as an alternative substitute for heavy cream.

The nutritional analyses were prepared using the *Nutrition Data System for Research* (NDSR). When a choice is given, the analyses are based on the first listed ingredient or quantity. Optional ingredients are not included. Phytoestrogens are valued by the sum of "isoflavones or similar."

Key to Abbreviations:

Cal.	Calories (Kilocalories)
GI	Glycemic Index
Prot.	Protein
Carb.	Carbohydrate
SFA	Saturated Fatty Acids
MUFA	Monounsaturated Fatty Acids
PUFA	Polyunsaturated Fatty Acids
Calc.	Calcium
Sod.	Sodium
Pot.	Potassium

1. Seibel MM. The soy solution for menopause: an alternative to estrogen. New York: Simon & Schuster; 2003.

2. U.S. Department of Health and Human Services. Dietary guidelines for Americans, 2005. Available at: www.health.gov/dietaryguidelines/dga2005/document/pdf/DGA2005.pdf (accessed July 26, 2009).

3. Schultze M, Manson J, Ludwig D, et al. Sugar-sweetened beverages, weight gain, and incidence of type 2 diabetes in young and middle-aged women. JAMA 2004;292(8):927–34.

4. Tordoff MG, Alleva AM. Effect of drinking soda sweetened with aspartame or high-fructose corn syrup on food intake and body weight. Am J Clin Nutr 1990;51(6):963–9.

5. The University of Sydney. The glycemic index and GI database. Available at: www.glycemicindex.com (accessed July 26, 2009).

6. Seibel MM, Khalsa HK. A Woman's Book of Yoga. New York: Penguin Putnam; 2002.

7. Roberts SB, Russ P, Heyman MB, et al. Control of food intake in older men. JAMA 1994;272:601–6.

8. University of Massachusetts Medical School. Center for Integrative Medicine. Omega-3 fatty acids (fish oils). Available at: www.umassmed.edu/uploadedfiles/Omega3FattyAcids.pdf (accessed July 20, 2009).

9. University of Massachusetts Medical School. Lipids: What do my cholesterol levels mean? Available at: www.umassmed.edu/healthyheart/tipsheets/lipids.aspx (accessed July 20, 2009).

10. United States Department of Agriculture (USDA). MyPyramid.gov: Steps to a healthier you. Available at: www.mypyramid.gov (accessed July 20, 2009).

11. Centers for Disease Control (CDC)/National Center for Health Statistics (NCHS). National Health and Nutrition Examination Survey (NHANES). NCHS data brief number 17, May 2009. Available at: www.cdc.gov/nchs/data/databriefs/db17.htm (accessed August 3, 2009).

12. United States Department of Agriculture (USDA). Inside the pyramid: What counts as a cup of vegetables? Available at: www.mypyramid.gov/pyramid/vegetables_counts_table.html (accessed July 20, 2009).

13. United States Department of Agriculture (USDA). Inside the pyramid: What counts as a cup of fruit? Available at: www.mypyramid.gov/pyramid/fruits_counts_table.html (accessed July 20, 2009).

14. Centers for Disease Control (CDC). Fruit & vegetable benefits. Available at: www.fruitsandveggiesmatter.gov/benefits/nutrient_guide.html (accessed July 20, 2009).

15. Centers for Disease Control (CDC). How to use fruits and vegetables to help manage your weight. Available at: www.cdc.gov/healthyweight/healthy_eating/fruits_vegetables.html (accessed July 20, 2009).

16. University of Massachusetts Medical School. Center for Integrative Nutrition. Seven ways to size up your portions. Available at: www.umassmed.edu/uploadedfiles/SevenWaysToSizeUpYourPortions.pdf (accessed July 27, 2009).

17. Ornish D, Fletcher J, Fullsack J-M, Roe HR. Everyday cooking with Dr. Dean Ornish. New York: HarperCollins; 1996.

Appetizers
and Side Dishes

spinach, basil, and red pepper wraps

 Chef Goldfarb has combined delightful flavors and fresh vegetables to make one of the best wraps in the world.

4 large whole-wheat or flour tortillas

8 teaspoons mango chutney or honey mustard, divided

24 basil leaves, divided

8 slices reduced fat Cheddar cheese, divided

1 red bell pepper, seeded, ribs removed, and cut into long, thin strips, divided

4 cups baby spinach, divided

Heat the tortillas in the microwave (some people prefer to heat them over an open flame on the stovetop for a few seconds) until they are warm and soft.

Spread 2 teaspoons of the mango chutney or honey mustard on one side of each tortilla. Top the spread on each wrap with 6 basil leaves, placed from one end to the other. Top the basil with 2 slices of cheese, ¼ of the red bell pepper (lay the strips across the middle of the tortilla so you can roll it up), and 1 cup of the spinach.

Roll the wraps as tightly as possible, and slice them in half or into bite-sized pieces before serving.

Yield: 4 servings

—Aviva Goldfarb

Per serving: 355 Cal.; 48 GI; 16g Prot.; 25g Carb.; 7g SFA; 6g MUFA; 1g PUFA; 0.3g Omega-3; 376mg Calc.; 667mg Sod.; 397mg Pot.; 2mg Iron; 0mg Phytoestrogen; 4g Fiber

> **To lose or control weight . . .**
> Replace 2 ounces of the cheese and 2 ounces of the meat in your sandwich, wrap, or burrito with lettuce, tomatoes, cucumbers, or onions.

goat cheese monte cristo

 In the quest to eat healthier, more and more people have become interested in goat cheese. Goat cheese is highly nutritious and great for women who have lactose intolerance.

Thinly slice the brioche into 28 slices. Combine the cheeses, herbs, and salt and pepper to taste in a mixing bowl. Spread the cheese mixture on 14 slices of the brioche, and then place a slice of ham on top of the cheese and dust with the flour. Brush with the beaten eggs and sprinkle with the panko. Cover the sandwich halves with the remaining slices of brioche.

Heat the oil in a deep skillet and deep-fry the sandwiches, a few at a time, turning them over to brown on each side. Set aside to drain on paper towels. Serve hot.

Yield: 28 sandwiches

—Chef Neal Fraser

Per serving: 181 Cal.; 67 GI; 10g Prot.; 10g Carb.; 7g SFA; 3g MUFA; 0.5g PUFA; 0.02g Omega-3; 188mg Calc.; 188mg Sod.; 68mg Pot.; 1.5mg Iron; 0mg Phytoestrogen; 0.5g Fiber

1 brioche loaf

½ pound soft goat cheese, crumbled

½ pound aged goat cheese (drunken goat cheese), grated

1½ to 2 cups chopped mixed herbs (parsley, chives, chervil, thyme)

Salt and pepper

14 slices of serrano ham

All-purpose flour

2 eggs, lightly beaten

Panko

Oil for deep-frying

nori rolls

 Nori rolls are good party hors d'oeuvres. They also make a great meal when served with salad greens and grilled shiitake mushrooms.

5 sheets of nori

2½ cups cooked brown rice, divided (1 cup brown rice cooked in 1¾ cups water yields 2½ cups cooked rice)

2½ teaspoons wasabi paste (or wasabi powder, diluted according to package directions), divided

1 avocado, peeled and cut into small cubes

1 cucumber, peeled, julienned, and cut into 1-inch lengths

3 carrots, peeled, julienned, and cut into 1-inch lengths

5 scallions, julienned, and cut into 1-inch lengths

Place a sheet of nori on a bamboo sushi rolling mat. Moisten your hands with water and spread ¾ cup of brown rice evenly over the surface of the nori sheet, leaving a bare 1½-inch-wide strip along the top edge. Spread ½ teaspoon of the wasabi paste over about one-third of the sheet, and place a strip each of the vegetables on top. Starting at the bottom, roll the nori sheet, wrapping the vegetables, toward the top, using steady pressure. You may need to moisten the edge slightly to seal. Repeat with the remaining nori, rice, wasabi, and vegetables.

Wrap each roll in plastic wrap and refrigerate until serving. To serve, cut each roll with a sharp knife into 5 pieces.

Yield: 25 nori rolls

—*Benay Vynerib*

Per serving: 113 Cal.; 50 GI; 3g Prot.; 19g Carb.; 0.4g SFA; 2g MUFA; 0.5g PUFA; 0.03g Omega-3; 30mg Calc.; 266mg Sod.; 279mg Pot.; 1mg Iron; 0mg Phytoestrogen; 5g Fiber

caribbean-style black bean and rice salad

 This lovely appetizer is easy to prepare. It can also be served as a luncheon dish. Chopped cooked and cooled shrimp makes a lovely addition to this recipe.

To make the dressing, whisk the olive oil, vinegar, mustard, cumin, and garlic in a small bowl until well blended. Season to taste with salt and pepper.

To make the salad, combine the beans, rice, peppers, and green onions in a large bowl. Toss the salad with enough dressing to moisten and season with salt and pepper to taste.

Yield: 6 to 8 servings

—*Cynthia Niles*

Per serving: 553 Cal.; 54 GI; 13g Prot.; 62g Carb.; 4g SFA; 20g MUFA; 4g PUFA; 0.4g Omega-3; 123mg Calc.; 888mg Sod.; 662mg Pot.; 5mg Iron; 0.3mg Phytoestrogen; 13g Fiber

DRESSING:

½ cup olive oil

¼ cup white wine vinegar

1 tablespoon Dijon mustard

1 tablespoon ground cumin

1 tablespoon minced garlic

Salt and pepper

BEANS AND RICE:

1 (15-ounce) can black beans, drained and rinsed

2½ cups cooked white rice (about 1 cup raw), cooled

¾ cup chopped red bell pepper

¾ cup chopped yellow bell pepper

¾ cup chopped green onion

Salt and pepper

stuffed zucchini

 This is an easy-to-prepare recipe using an abundant summer vegetable.

2 medium-large zucchinis

3 to 4 slices of whole-wheat bread, diced small

½ cup reduced-fat shredded sharp Cheddar cheese

½ teaspoon salt

¼ teaspoon pepper

¼ teaspoon dried oregano

1/8 teaspoon garlic powder

3 tablespoons olive oil

Preheat the oven to 425°F. Lightly grease a medium-sized baking dish.

Trim both ends of each zucchini, slice in half lengthwise, and cut each slice in half crosswise. Place the zucchini pieces in a large saucepan with water and parboil until tender, but not mushy. Drain and cool, and then scoop out the seeds.

Combine the bread, cheese, salt, pepper, oregano, garlic powder, and butter in a large bowl. Mix well and stuff into the hollow of each piece of zucchini. Place the zucchini in the greased baking dish and bake for 15 minutes. Serve hot.

Yield: 6 servings

—*Cynthia Niles*

Per serving: 209 Cal.; 68 GI; 7g Prot.; 16 g Carb.; 3g SFA; 8g MUFA; 1g PUFA; 0.1g Omega-3; 120mg Calc.; 368mg Sod.; 374mg Pot.; 1mg Iron; 0.05mg Phytoestrogen; 3g Fiber

black bean salsa

 This is a wonderful salsa for a buffet, and it can be prepared in a jiffy. Serve chilled.

In a large mixing bowl, combine the beans, peppers, onion, and cilantro. In small mixing bowl, whisk together the vinegar, garlic, lime juice, and salt and pepper to taste, and then pour over the black bean mixture and toss to mix well. Chill in the refrigerator and serve with tortilla chips.

Yield: 6 to 8 servings

—*Cynthia Niles*

Per serving: 56 Cal.; 40 GI; 2g Prot.; 11g Carb.; 0.03g SFA; 0.04 g MUFA; 0.15 g PUFA; 0.05g Omega-3; 28mg Calc.; 113mg Sod.; 170mg Pot.; 1mg Iron; 0mg Phytoestrogen; 3g Fiber

1 (16-ounce) can black beans, rinsed and drained

1 red bell pepper, cut into small bite-sized pieces

1 green bell pepper, cut into small bite-sized pieces

1 red onion, cut into small bite-sized pieces

½ cup chopped cilantro

½ cup balsamic vinegar

2 tablespoons crushed garlic

2 tablespoons lime juice

Salt and pepper

Cocktail party advice
If you are going to a cocktail party, always eat something solid before you get there so you won't go overboard on the appetizers.

sesame tamari tofu

 This is a delicious dish that is rich in phytoestrogens, which help with hot flashes and bone health. And it's easy to make.

Cooking spray

1 (15-ounce) package firm or extra-firm tofu

2 tablespoons tamari

1 tablespoon crushed or whole sesame seeds

2 green onions, chopped

Preheat the oven to 350°F. Spray a medium baking dish with cooking spray.

Slice the tofu into 10 to 12 slabs and put them in a gallon-sized sealable plastic bag. Add the tamari; seal the bag, squeezing out air; and turn to coat the tofu evenly. Refrigerate for at least 15 to 20 minutes, turning the bag occasionally.

Place the tofu in the prepared baking dish and sprinkle with the sesame seeds. Bake for 20 to 25 minutes, or until lightly browned, turning once or twice for even browning. Top with the green onions and serve hot.

Yield: 4 servings

—*Hari Kaur Khalsa*

Per serving: 115 Cal.; 23 GI; 11g Prot.; 3.5g Carb.; 0.7g SFA; 5g MUFA; 1g PUFA; 0g Omega-3; 213mg Calc.; 458mg Sod.; 184mg Pot.; 2.5mg Iron; 24mg Phytoestrogen; 1g Fiber

edamame

 Enjoy this simple recipe. Edamame is great for reducing hot flashes and keeping bones strong, and it is an excellent source of protein.

Place the soybeans in a medium saucepan and add the water to cover. Bring to a boil over high heat and boil for 10 to 15 minutes. Drain and chill in the refrigerator. Arrange the beans in a fanned-out pattern on a serving platter and sprinkle with salt. Diners can shell the beans themselves as they eat them. (The pods are inedible.)

½ pound soybeans in the pod

2 cups water

1/8 teaspoon salt

Yield: 4 servings

—Dr. Mache's Kitchen

Per serving: 80 Cal.; 50 GI; 7g Prot.; 6g Carb.; 0.4g SFA; 0.6g MUFA; 2g PUFA; 0.2g Omega-3; 82mg Calc.; 79mg Sod.; 306mg Pot.; 1mg Iron; 10mg Phytoestrogen; 2.3g Fiber

fresh green soybeans

 Enjoy this healthy, quick vegan recipe. It's a perfect dish for Red Hot Mamas!

1 pound fresh soybeans in the pod

4 cups boiling water

1 cup cold water

1/8 teaspoon salt

Put the soybeans in a large saucepan, add the boiling water to cover the soybeans, and let stand for 5 minutes. Drain the water. Break the pods open and remove the beans, discarding the pods. Put the beans back into the same saucepan, add the cold water, and bring to a gentle boil over medium-high heat. Boil for 15 to 20 minutes, or until the beans are tender. Sprinkle with the salt and serve hot.

Yield: 3 (½-cup) servings

—*Dr. Mache's Kitchen*

Per serving: 160 Cal.; 50 GI; 14g Prot.; 12g Carb.; 0.8g SFA; 1g MUFA; 3g PUFA; 0.4g Omega-3; 164mg Calc.; 87mg Sod.; 611mg Pot.; 3mg Iron; 20mg Phytoestrogen; 5g Fiber

What are phytoestrogens?
Phytoestrogens are plant foods that have a chemical structure similar to estrogen, so they work in the body like a weak estrogen. The major phytoestrogen groups are isoflavones (found mostly in soy), flavones, coumestans, and lignans (found mostly in flaxseeds).

roasted soy nuts

 This is a tasty appetizer that makes a healthy snack for those afternoon cravings. Soy nuts help reduce hot flashes and keep bones strong.

Place the soybeans in a medium bowl, cover with water, and soak for about 3 hours. (Choose a bowl that will allow the beans to double in size.)

Preheat the oven to 350°F and spray a cookie sheet with cooking spray.

Drain and spread the soybeans on the prepared cookie sheet and roast for about 45 minutes, until browned, stirring every 10 to 15 minutes.

Lightly salt to taste and store in an airtight container; they should keep for a month at room temperature.

Yield: 4 servings

—*Dr. Mache's Kitchen*

Per serving: 105 Cal.; 15 GI; 9g Prot.; 8g Carb.; 0.7g SFA; 1g MUFA; 3g PUFA; 0.3g Omega-3; 33mg Calc.; 123mg Sod.; 317mg Pot.; 1mg Iron; 30mg Phytoestrogen; 4g Fiber

1 cup shelled fresh soybeans

2 cups water

Cooking spray

1/8 teaspoon salt

pan-seared sardines, slow-cooked grains, swiss chard, golden raisins, pine nuts, and smoked paprika

 This dish is elegantly prepared with a fantastic combination of ingredients. It is a must for sardine lovers!

SLOW-COOKED GRAINS AND SWISS CHARD:

2/3 cup wheat berries (or any other kind of wheat, such as bulgur)

1 quart water

½ cup French lentils (or any other kind of lentils)

2 tablespoons extra-virgin olive oil

2 cloves of garlic, minced

1 cup chopped Vidalia onion

1 leaf of lemon thyme, chopped

3 quarts chicken broth

1½ cups chopped red Swiss chard

Pinch of cinnamon

2 tablespoons chopped cilantro

1 teaspoon salt

1 teaspoon pepper

PAN-SEARED SARDINES:

12 sardines (3 ounces each without heads, guts, and scales) (substitute with any other fish high in omega-3 fats, such as salmon or mackerel)

To make the slow-cooked grains and Swiss chard, soak the wheat berries in the water overnight. The next day, heat the olive oil in a large, heavy saucepan and sauté the onion, garlic, and lemon thyme until the vegetables are tender. Add the wheat berries and chicken broth to the saucepan and bring to a boil over high heat. Reduce the heat and simmer, covered, for about 25 minutes. Add the lentils and more chicken broth if necessary and continue to simmer, covered, for 12 more minutes. Add the chard and cook, covered, for another 5 minutes, and then stir in the cinnamon, cilantro, salt, and pepper. Cover and set aside on the stove top to keep warm.

To make the pan-seared sardines, drizzle the sardines with the olive oil and sprinkle with a pinch of salt and pepper. Preheat a large skillet until it turns very hot. Add the sardines and cook them for about 1½ minutes on each side. Remove the sardines to a bowl and set aside. Do not wash out the skillet.

To make the golden raisins, pine nuts, and smoked paprika, using the same skillet (unwashed) as the sardines were cooked in, heat the olive oil over medium heat and add the raisins, pine nuts, and tomatoes and sauté for 1 minute. Turn the heat off and stir in the vinegar, parsley, paprika, and salt and pepper to taste.

To serve, warm 4 individual serving plates. Spoon a portion of the hot grains and chard mixture onto each plate and top each with 3 sardines. Pour the sautéed raisins and paprika mixture over the sardines. Garnish each serving with the chopped parsley and a few grindings of pepper and decorate each with a few sprigs of cilantro. Serve hot.

Yield: 4 servings

—Chef Luis Bollo

Per serving: 1,063 Cal.; 42 GI; 92g Prot.; 53g Carb.; 8g SFA; 26g MUFA; 13g PUFA; 7g Omega-3; 151mg Calc.; 1,295mg Sod.; 3,095mg Pot.; 10mg Iron; 7mg Phytoestrogen; 11g Fiber

1 tablespoon extra-virgin olive oil

Salt and pepper

GOLDEN RAISINS, PINE NUTS, AND SMOKED PAPRIKA:

4 tablespoons extra-virgin olive oil

¼ cup golden raisins

2 tablespoons pine nuts

8 small grape tomatoes, halved

1 tablespoon white balsamic vinegar (or any white wine vinegar)

1 tablespoon chopped Italian parsley

1 teaspoon smoked Spanish paprika (or any other paprika)

Salt and pepper

GARNISHES:

Chopped parsley

Pepper

Cilantro sprigs

Whole grain goodness

Make half your grains whole and avoid refined grains because they remove the bran and germ portions of the grain kernel, which also removes the fiber. If you do eat refined grains, make sure they are enriched, meaning the makers put back in the B vitamins and iron that are removed during the refining process. The fiber in whole grains helps you eat more slowly and fill up naturally, and this helps prevent overeating.

stuffed bell peppers

 Stuffed peppers are a great meal that won't leave you feeling stuffed. If you like a meat dish, the ground turkey will satisfy that craving perfectly. For many people, one pepper half is just the right portion size, but two will satisfy even the hearty eaters in your family. Goes great with brown rice and a salad.

5 bell peppers (red, yellow, green, orange), halved and seeded

1 tablespoon canola oil

1 large onion, chopped

1 pound lean ground turkey

2 tablespoons cooked brown rice

1 (8-ounce) and 1 (15-ounce) can tomato sauce

Salt and pepper

Preheat the oven to 350°F.

Place the 10 bell pepper halves facing up in a 9 by 13-inch baking dish.

Heat the canola oil in a small skillet over medium heat. Add the onion and sauté until the onion is tender. In a mixing bowl, combine the turkey, sautéed onions, rice, 8-ounce can of tomato sauce, a dash of pepper, and a pinch of salt and mix well. Stuff the peppers with the meat mixture. Pour the 15-ounce can of tomato sauce over the peppers and cover the baking dish with aluminum foil. Place in the oven and bake for 1½ hours.

Yield: 8 servings

—*Dr. Mache's Kitchen*

Per serving: 248 Cal.; 53 GI; 25g Prot.; 18g Carb.; 2g SFA; 4g MUFA; 2g PUFA; 0.3g Omega-3; 52mg Calc.; 849mg Sod.; 944mg Pot.; 3mg Iron; 0mg Phytoestrogen; 5g Fiber

breakfast to go (and we mean "to go")

 For a mild and delicious stimulant, this is clearly "the way to go."

Soak the almonds and the pitted prunes overnight in 1 cup of water. In the morning, blend the mixture in a food processor until liquefied as completely as possible. Drink as a morning drink. (Don't be surprised if the almonds have begun to sprout after 6 hours of soaking.)

12 almonds (with skins)

6 pitted prunes

Yield: 1 serving

—*Dr. Mache's Kitchen*

Per serving: 222 Cal.; 29 GI; 4g Prot.; 40g Carb.; 0.6g SFA; 4.5g MUFA; 2g PUFA; 0.01g Omega-3; 64mg Calc.; 1mg Sod.; 522mg Pot.; 1mg Iron; 0mg Phytoestrogen; 6g Fiber

eggplant pakoras

 This is a popular Indian dish that contains lots of good vegetables and seasonings. It can be served with a salad for a delicious light meal.

1 tablespoon caraway seeds

1 teaspoon oregano seeds

1 teaspoon cardamom seeds

½ teaspoon ground cinnamon

2 teaspoons turmeric

2 teaspoons salt

1 teaspoon pepper

½ teaspoon ground cloves

2 cups chickpea flour

¾ cup onion juice or purée

½ cup milk

1/3 cup water

¼ cup honey

Vegetable oil or ghee for frying

1 eggplant, cut crosswise into 3/8-inch slices

In a large mixing bowl, combine the spices and seeds with the chickpea flour and mix well. Add the onion juice, milk, water, and honey and stir into a paste, mixing with a fork until smooth.

Heat the oil or ghee in a large skillet over medium-high heat. Dip the eggplant slices in the batter and fry them until golden brown. Transfer to paper towels to drain. Serve with ketchup or chutney.

Yield: 4 to 6 servings

—*Hari Kaur Khalsa*

Per serving: 263 Cal.; 57 GI; 11g Prot.; 47g Carb.; 0.8g SFA; 1g MUFA; 1g PUFA; 0.1g Omega-3; 88mg Calc.; 1,040mg Sod.; 720mg Pot.; 3mg Iron; 1mg Phytoestrogen; 10g Fiber

couscous with pumpkin, almonds, and dried apricots

 A versatile alternative to rice, couscous is quick and easy to cook.

Preheat the oven to 375°F.

In a large bowl, mix 2 tablespoons of the olive oil with the pumpkin and brown sugar and season to taste with salt. Spread on a baking sheet and bake in the oven for 20 minutes.

Heat the remaining 2 tablespoons of the olive oil in a saucepan over medium-high heat. Add the onions and sauté for 5 minutes. Add the garlic and sauté for 2 minutes more. Add the cinnamon and cloves and sauté for 1 minute longer. Add the chicken broth and heat through.

Place the couscous in a large metal bowl. Pour the hot broth mixture over the couscous and wrap the whole bowl with plastic wrap and let sit for 10 minutes. Remove the plastic wrap and fluff the couscous with a fork. Fold in the mint, rosemary, almonds, and apricots. Season as needed and serve.

Yield: 6 servings

—*Michelle Bernstein*

Per serving: 650 Cal.; 57 GI; 20g Prot.; 92g Carb.; 3g SFA; 15g MUFA; 4g PUFA; 0.14g Omega-3; 108mg Calc.; 278mg Sod.; 804mg Pot.; 3mg Iron; 0mg Phytoestrogen; 9g Fiber

4 tablespoons olive oil, divided

2 cups pumpkin, peeled, seeded, and diced small

1 tablespoon brown sugar

Salt

1 cup minced yellow onions

2 cloves of garlic, minced

¼ teaspoon ground cinnamon

Pinch of ground cloves

3 cups chicken broth

2 cups couscous

3 tablespoons finely chopped mint

¼ teaspoon finely chopped rosemary

½ cup chopped Marcona almonds

½ cup dried apricots, thinly sliced

kasha

This is a wonderful light meal when served with a salad. It also works well as a side dish.

1½ cups kasha (medium-sized buckwheat groats)

2 eggs

3 cups boiling water

1 tablespoon salt

4 tablespoons butter (½ stick)

1 onion, diced

Preheat the oven to 350°F.

Place the kasha in a shallow baking dish or pie pan. Stir in, but do not beat, the eggs until the kasha is coated. Bake with the oven door slightly ajar, until the grains are dry (about 25 minutes). Shake the pan and stir the kasha about every 5 minutes to keep the groats from sticking. Transfer the kasha to a large saucepan. Add the boiling water and salt. Cover and cook over moderate heat for 10 to 15 minutes. It may be necessary to add a little more water. (When done, the kasha will be tender and doubled in bulk, and all the cooking water absorbed.)

Heat the butter in a skillet over medium-high heat. Add the onion and sauté until browned, and then scrape the onion and butter into the kasha, stir, and serve.

Yield: 6 servings

—*Bubbie's Kitchen*

Per serving: 194 Cal.; 46 GI; 5g Prot.; 21g Carb.; 5g SFA; 3g MUFA; 1g PUFA; 0.06g Omega-3; 22mg Calc.; 853mg Sod.; 136mg Pot.; 1mg Iron; 0mg Phytoestrogen; 3g Fiber

mashed sweet potatoes and apples

 This recipe is a tasty alternative to traditional mashed or baked potato, and it goes well with roast chicken, turkey, or pork.

Bring a large saucepan of water to a boil over high heat. Add the whole sweet potatoes and boil briskly for 30 to 35 minutes, or until tender. Drain and let cool slightly.

In a large skillet with a lid, melt the 1 tablespoon of butter over medium heat. Add the onions and cook, stirring occasionally, for 6 to 8 minutes, or until golden and tender. Add the apples and water and cook, covered, over medium-low heat for 10 to 15 minutes, or until the apples are tender.

Preheat the oven to 375°F and grease a medium-sized baking dish.

Peel the potatoes (the skin should slip off), cut into chunks, and put into a large bowl. Add the 1½ teaspoons of butter, salt, pepper, nutmeg, and apple mixture and mash with a potato masher or the back of a spoon until smooth. Spoon the mixture into the greased baking dish and bake for 25 to 30 minutes. Garnish with dill or parsley and serve.

Yield: 8 servings

—*Cynthia Niles*

Per serving: 181 Cal.; 45 GI; 2g Prot.; 37g Carb.; 2g SFA; 1g MUFA; 0g PUFA; 0g Omega-3; 49mg Calc.; 160mg Sod.; 434mg Pot.; 1mg Iron; 0mg Phytoestrogen; 5g Fiber

2 pounds sweet potatoes (about 6 medium), left whole and unpeeled

1 tablespoon plus 1½ teaspoons butter

½ cup chopped onion

2 large Granny Smith apples, peeled, cored, and coarsely chopped (2½ cups)

2½ tablespoons water

¼ teaspoon salt

¼ teaspoon pepper

¼ teaspoon grated nutmeg

GARNISH:

Chopped dill or parsley

carrot-pineapple slaw

 A new way to prepare slaw, this recipe would complement any meal nicely.

1 cup diced fresh pineapple (or drained canned pineapple chunks, juice reserved)

½ cup raisins

1 (10-ounce) package of matchstick-cut carrots

2 tablespoons canola oil

2 tablespoons freshly squeezed lemon juice

2 tablespoons maple syrup

1 tablespoon fresh pineapple juice (if you use canned pineapple you can use the juice from the can)

2 tablespoons chopped Italian parsley

¼ teaspoon salt

1/8 teaspoon pepper

Combine the pineapple, raisins, and carrots in a large bowl. In a small bowl, combine the canola oil, lemon juice, maple syrup, and pineapple juice and whisk until well blended. Pour the oil mixture over the pineapple mixture and toss well. Add the parsley, salt, and pepper and toss well. Cover and chill before serving.

Yield: 6 (1-cup) servings

—*Cynthia Niles*

Per serving: 194 Cal.; 60 GI; 1.5g Prot.; 34g Carb.; 0.5g SFA; 4g MUFA; 2g PUFA; 0.6g Omega-3; 53mg Calc.; 203mg Sod.; 485mg Pot.; 1mg Iron; 0mg Phytoestrogen; 3g Fiber

Soups
and Stews

crab and sweet potato soup

 This soup is a never-ending delight that you can enjoy year round.

2 pounds sweet potatoes,
peeled and diced

½ yellow onion, diced

4 cloves of garlic, minced

1 tablespoon ground coriander

1 teaspoon salt

1 teaspoon ground nutmeg

½ teaspoon cayenne

½ teaspoon white pepper

2 cloves

8 cups water

1½ cups dry sherry

1 cup orange juice

¼ cup lemon juice

1 tablespoon hoisin sauce

1 pound crabmeat (claw)

Combine all the ingredients except the crab in a large saucepan. Cover and bring just to a boil over medium-high heat, and then reduce the heat and simmer, covered, for 20 to 30 minutes, until the potatoes are tender. Purée the soup in a food processor or with an immersion blender and return to the saucepan. Add the crabmeat and heat through. Serve hot.

Yield: 6 to 8 servings

—Chef Tres Hundertmark

Per serving: 235 Cal.; 50 GI; 14g Prot.; 30.5g Carb.; 0.2g SFA; 0.2g MUFA; 0.5g PUFA; 0.3g Omega-3; 116mg Calc.; 382mg Sod.; 564mg Pot.; 2mg Iron; 0.2mg Phytoestrogen; 3.3g Fiber

maine fiddlehead fern soup

 This wonderful and unusual soup can be enjoyed in the spring, when fiddleheads are in season. It is delicious and easy to prepare ahead of time.

Melt the butter in a saucepan over medium-high heat. Add the onion, garlic, and fiddleheads and sauté until the onions are translucent and the water has started to leach out of the vegetables. Sprinkle with the salt and a few grindings of white pepper. Add the vegetable broth and bring to a boil. Once boiling, add the milk and bring to a boil again. Remove from the heat and blend the soup in a high-speed bar blender or a food processor until smooth. Return to the saucepan, season to taste, and heat through. Pour into 4 individual soup bowls, top each with a teaspoon of crème fraîche, and serve.

Yield: 4 servings

—*Chef Jonathan Cartwright*

Per serving: 178 Cal.; 54 GI; 7g Prot.; 15g Carb.; 6g SFA; 3g MUFA; 0.4g PUFA; 0.04g Omega-3; 129mg Calc.; 1,103mg Sod.; 572mg Pot.; 2mg Iron; 0mg Phytoestrogen; 3g Fiber

3 tablespoons butter*

1 onion, chopped

1 clove of garlic

1 pound fiddleheads

2 teaspoons salt

White pepper

4 cups vegetable broth

1 cup milk

4 teaspoons crème fraîche

To reduce the saturated fat content in this recipe, a butter substitute such as Smart Balance can be used.

iced watermelon and maine blueberry soup

 This tasty soup is perfect for a luncheon on a warm summer day, followed by a green salad and a light dessert.

1 (2-pound) watermelon

1 pound blueberries

2 cups muscat wine (or any sweet dessert wine, or orange juice)

2 cups champagne, chilled

Peel, dice, and seed the watermelon. In a liquidizer or food processor, blend the blueberries, watermelon, and wine until smooth. Strain through a fine strainer and chill. Just before serving, add the chilled champagne.

Yield: 4 servings

—*Chef Jonathan Cartwright*

Per serving: 311 Cal.; 57 GI; 2g Prot.; 29g Carb.; 0g SFA; 0g MUFA; 0.1g PUFA; 0g Omega-3; 40mg Calc.; 16mg Sod.; 420mg Pot.; 1mg Iron; 0mg Phytoestrogen; 2g Fiber

Fruits are really good for you.

They are a great source of vitamins, minerals, and fiber. Eat fruit as snacks and desserts. It doesn't matter if they are fresh, canned, frozen, or dried and may be whole, cut up, or puréed. But remember to buy dried fruits that are processed without sugar. The whole fruit has much fewer calories than the fruit juice.

roasted sweet potato and apple soup

 This soup evokes images of oak furniture and a roaring fireplace at an old country inn.

Preheat the oven to 450°F.

Put the sweet potatoes, apples, onion, and garlic in a roasting pan. Toss them with the olive oil and a few shakes of salt and pepper to taste, if using. Place in the oven and roast, tossing every 10 minutes, until the vegetables and apples are tender, about 30 minutes.

Add just enough broth to cover the vegetable and apple mixture and purée in a food processor (or in the roasting pan using an immersion blender). Add more broth if necessary to reach a consistency that is smooth and not too thick. (If you are using a food processor, you will probably need to purée the soup in two batches.)

Warm the soup over low heat in a saucepan until ready to serve, or refrigerate for up to 1 day or freeze for up to 3 months. Stir in the sour cream at the table for a creamier taste, if desired.

Variation: Add ¼ to ½ teaspoon of ground ginger or 1 tablespoon of fresh grated ginger to the roasted vegetables before blending, or ¼ to ½ teaspoon of ground chipotle chili pepper for a spicy bite.

Yield: 6 servings (about 1½ cups each)

—*Aviva Goldfarb*

Per serving: 145 Cal.; 54 GI; 4g Prot.; 23g Carb.; 0.6g SFA; 3g MUFA; 0.5g PUFA; 0.03g Omega-3; 71mg Calc.; 427mg Sod.; 353mg Pot.; 1mg Iron; 0mg Phytoestrogen; 2g Fiber

2 medium sweet potatoes, peeled and cut into medium chunks

1 firm apple, such as Gala or Jonagold, peeled, cored, and quartered

1 medium yellow onion, peeled and quartered

2 cloves of garlic

2 tablespoons olive oil

Salt and pepper (optional)

3 to 4 cups low-sodium chicken or vegetable broth

¾ cup non-fat sour cream for serving (optional)

rocky mountain minestrone

This delicious Italian minestrone soup is filled with hearty and healthy vegetables and beans. It makes a great inexpensive family meal or side dish. Often soup is based on the strength of the broth being used. If you have time to make a good strong chicken broth, great, but if you don't, be sure to add a bouillon cube to intensify the flavor of store-bought broth. If you use store-bought broth, it can be salty, so season accordingly.

3 tablespoons extra-virgin olive oil

1 large white onion, chopped

¼ cup all-purpose flour

1 cup dry sherry (or dry red wine)

2 large potatoes, peeled and cut into ½-inch cubes

1 small head white cabbage, cored and chopped into bite-sized pieces

2 ribs of celery, chopped

2 zucchinis, cut into ½-inch cubes

2 large tomatoes, chopped

1 cup cooked white beans (you can use canned, but home cooked is better)

1 cup cooked chickpeas (you can use canned, but home cooked is better)

Chicken or vegetable broth

Heat the olive oil in a large saucepan over medium heat. Add the onions and sauté until translucent but not brown. Whisk in the flour to make a roux (this is for thickening).

To the saucepan, add the sherry, potatoes, cabbage, celery, zucchinis, tomatoes, and beans. Add enough broth to cover and bring to a boil, skimming off any froth that rises to the surface.

Once all the froth has been skimmed off, reduce the heat to low and add salt and pepper to taste (remember, you can add more, but you can't take it out, so season as you go). Add the basil, bay leaf, and parsley and simmer, covered, until the vegetables are tender but not mushy.

When the vegetables are done, add the pasta or rice if desired. Before serving, dribble the top of each serving with extra-virgin olive oil or 1 tablespoon of pesto.

Yield: 6 main dish servings or 12 side dish servings

—Antonio Laudisio

Per serving: 513 Cal.; 51 GI; 16g Prot.; 60g Carb.; 4g SFA; 20g MUFA; 3g PUFA; 0.3g Omega-3; 130mg Calc.; 1,121mg Sod.; 1,329mg Pot.; 5mg Iron; 0.2mg Phytoestrogen; 10g Fiber

Salt and pepper

1 teaspoon chopped basil (or ¼ teaspoon dried)

1 bay leaf

½ bunch of parsley

½ pound pasta shells (or 1 cup rice) (optional)

GARNISH:

Extra-virgin olive oil or pesto

lentil soup

 Italians eat lentils on New Year's, as soon after midnight as possible. The lentils symbolize coins and are supposed to help bring prosperity in the New Year.

6 cups water

1 teaspoon salt

2¼ cups lentils

3 carrots, pared and chopped

2 ribs of celery, chopped

1 onion, finely chopped

¼ cup extra-virgin olive oil

1 clove of garlic, peeled

1 ounce anchovy fillets in oil, drained

1 (16-ounce) can tomatoes, chopped

Salt and pepper

Handful of torn basil

Handful of chopped Italian parsley

Extra-virgin olive oil for drizzling

Put the water and salt in an 8-quart saucepan. Add the lentils, carrots, celery, and onion and cook over medium heat for 10 minutes.

In a separate large saucepan, warm the olive oil over low heat. Add the garlic clove and cook until it becomes golden brown. Remove the garlic and add the anchovies, tomatoes, and salt and pepper to taste. Stir in the basil.

Drain the lentils and reserve the cooking water. Pour the lentils into the tomato mixture, gradually adding enough cooking water to make a thick soup. Cook over medium heat until the lentils are al dente (approximately 30 minutes). Sprinkle the parsley over the soup, drizzle a small amount of olive oil over top, and serve.

Yield: 4 servings

—*Karen's Cucina*

Per serving: 494 Cal.; 24 GI; 32g Prot.; 75g Carb.; 1g SFA; 6g MUFA; 2g PUFA; 0.3g Omega-3; 151mg Calc.; 478mg Sod.; 1,661mg Pot.; 12mg Iron; 0mg Phytoestrogen; 21g Fiber

angel hair pasta, chickpea, escarole, and sausage soup

 A steamy bowl of this highly flavorful soup will comfort you for the entire day.

Heat the olive oil in a large saucepan over medium heat. Add the onions, celery, and rosemary and sauté for 8 minutes. Then add the sausage and sauté until browned. Add the broth, water, beans, escarole, and tomato paste and bring to a boil over medium-high heat, and then reduce the heat and simmer, covered, for 25 minutes. Add the pasta and simmer, covered, for an additional 10 minutes, just until the pasta is al dente. Add salt and pepper to taste. Serve garnished with the freshly grated Parmesan cheese.

Yield: 4 servings

--Karen's Cucina

Per serving: 578 Cal.; 46 GI; 64g Prot.; 26g Carb ; 6g SFA; 12g MUFA; 4g PUFA; 0.3g Omega-3; 159mg Calc.; 1,907mg Sod.; 917mg Pot.; 6mg Iron; 2mg Phytoestrogen; 10g Fiber

3 tablespoons extra-virgin olive oil

½ cup chopped onions

1 rib of celery, chopped

2 tablespoons chopped rosemary

Pinch of crushed red pepper flakes

4 cloves of garlic, thinly sliced

2 medium Italian sweet sausages, casings removed and meat crumbled

4 cups beef broth

3 cups water

1 (15-ounce) can ceci beans

1 small head escarole, washed and chopped

4 tablespoons tomato paste

4 ounces angel hair pasta, broken into 1-inch pieces

Salt and pepper

Freshly grated Parmesan cheese

chicken soup with pasta

 This is a great soup recipe made with a beautiful blend of homemade chicken broth and vegetables that are in perfect harmony with the pasta.

1 (3½-pound) broiler-fryer chicken

Chicken giblets

2 medium carrots, pared

1 large parsnip, pared

1 onion

2 ribs of celery

2 celery tops

3 sprigs of Italian parsley

1 leek

Cold water

1 tablespoon salt

12 peppercorns

3 cups acini di pepe pasta

Freshly grated Parmesan cheese

In a large casserole, combine the chicken, giblets, carrots, parsnip, onion, and celery. Tie the celery tops, parsley, and leek together with string and add to casserole. Add enough cold water to cover the chicken and vegetables. Heat slowly to boiling, skimming off any froth that rises to the surface. Add the salt and peppercorns; reduce the heat; and simmer, covered, for 1½ hours, until the meat starts to fall off the bones. Remove the meat and vegetables from the broth and discard the bundle of greens that were tied with string. When cool enough to handle, take the meat off the bones, chop the vegetables, and put the chicken and vegetables back into the broth.

In a saucepan, cook the pasta al dente according to the package instructions. Drain the pasta and add it to the chicken soup. Serve topped with freshly grated Parmesan cheese.

Yield: 4 servings

—*Karen's Cucina*

Per serving: 857 Cal.; 52 GI; 97g Prot.; 57g Carb.; 6g SFA; 8g MUFA; 6g PUFA; 0.4g Omega-3; 109mg Calc.; 501mg Sod.; 1,163mg Pot.; 7.5mg Iron; 0mg Phytoestrogen; 6g Fiber

red hot mamas minestrone soup

Mmmmm . . . nothing better than minestrone soup for a Red Hot Mama. This is a simple, satisfying soup stocked with fresh vegetables.

Place the shin of beef, salt, and water in a large saucepan. Cover and bring to a boil, skimming off any froth that rises to the surface. Reduce the heat and add the carrots, celery, onion, parsley, and bay leaf. Simmer, uncovered, for 3 hours. Remove the beef and carrots and set aside. Strain the broth (there should be about 8 cups). In the same saucepan, combine the broth, tomatoes, chickpeas, green beans, peas, cabbage, spaghetti, and salt and pepper to taste. Bring to a boil, then reduce the heat and simmer, covered, for 45 minutes. Meanwhile, slice the carrots and remove the beef from the bone and add to the simmering soup near the end of cooking. Serve hot.

Yield: 4 servings

—*Karen's Cucina*

Per serving: 950 Cal.; 46 GI; 107g Prot.; 91g Carb.; 5g SFA; 6g MUFA; 3g PUFA; 0.1g Omega-3; 239mg Calc.; 725mg Sod.; 1,937mg Pot.; 16mg Iron; 2mg Phytoestrogen; 19g Fiber

1 (3-pound) shin of beef

1 tablespoon salt

4 quarts water

5 carrots, pared

2 ribs of celery, chopped

1 onion, quartered

5 sprigs of Italian parsley

1 bay leaf

1 (16-ounce) can tomatoes

1 (20-ounce) can chickpeas, undrained

1 (10-ounce) package frozen cut green beans

1 (10-ounce) package frozen peas

2 cups chopped cabbage

¼ pound spaghetti, broken into 1-inch pieces

Salt and pepper

pasta and bean soup (pasta e fagioli)

 Pasta e fagioli is a real comfort soup. There are a tremendous number of local variations of this soup in Italy. This particular version is one of Karen's favorite family recipes from Sicily.

¼ cup extra-virgin olive oil

3 cloves of garlic, minced

1 onion, chopped

1 rib of celery, diced

3 tablespoons tomato paste

1/3 cup pancetta, chopped

6 tablespoons minced rosemary

½ teaspoon dried basil

Salt and pepper

2 cups canned chicken broth

2 cups canned cannellini beans, drained

½ pound pasta

½ cup freshly grated Parmigiano-Reggiano cheese

Heat the olive oil in a large saucepan over medium-low heat. Add the garlic, onions, celery, tomato paste, pancetta, rosemary, basil, and salt and pepper to taste and sauté for 8 minutes. Add the broth and bring it to a boil, then reduce the heat and simmer, covered, for 10 minutes. Add the beans and simmer, covered, for another 15 minutes.

Cook the pasta al dente according to the package instructions, drain, and add to the soup. If the soup is too thick, add a little water. Add salt and pepper to taste and serve topped with the freshly grated cheese.

Yield: 4 servings

—*Karen's Cucina*

Per serving: 607 Cal.; 42 GI; 28g Prot.; 75g Carb.; 5g SFA; 12g MUFA; 2.5g PUFA; 0.2g Omega-3; 284mg Calc.; 1,442mg Sod.; 897mg Pot.; 6mg Iron; 0.2mg Phytoestrogen; 9g Fiber

piquillo pepper and tomato soup

 This inventive soup is excellent, and a cup of it often starts a great meal.

Preheat the oven to 350°F.

Put the tomatoes in a roasting pan and roast for about 1 hour, or until slightly charred.

In a large, heavy-bottomed saucepan, heat the butter over medium-high heat. Add the onions and sauté until tender. Add the carrots, garlic, and paprika and sauté until the vegetables are tender. Stir in the charred tomatoes and peppers, and then pour in the chicken broth. Reduce the heat and simmer, covered, for 2 hours. When the soup is cooked, stir in the saffron and season with salt and pepper to taste, and then blend it in a food processor. Strain the soup through a fine strainer, return it to the saucepan, and then stir in the saffron and season it with salt and pepper to taste. Heat through and serve.

Yield: 8 to 10 servings

—Chef Neal Fraser

Per serving: 190 Cal.; 52 GI; 12g Prot.; 18g Carb.; 4g SFA; 3g MUFA; 2g PUFA; 0.2g Omega-3; 105mg Calc.; 690mg Sod.; 570mg Pot.; 4mg Iron; 0mg Phytoestrogen; 5g Fiber

1 (16-ounce) can plum tomatoes

1 (16-ounce) can Roma tomatoes

2 ounces butter (½ stick)

½ cup chopped yellow onions

1 large carrot

2 cloves of garlic

6 canned piquillo peppers (or 2 small whole roasted red bell peppers)

8 cups chicken broth

2 teaspoons smoked paprika

Pinch of saffron

Salt and pepper

chilled tomato soup

 This wonderful cold soup is easy to prepare and it has an abundance of flavors.

9 vine-ripe tomatoes, peeled, seeded, and diced

1 medium red onion, diced

5 cloves of garlic, crushed

¼ cup chopped marjoram

½ cup red wine vinegar

2 teaspoons ground cumin

2 teaspoons ground coriander

2 teaspoons yellow curry powder

2 teaspoons paprika

3 cups tomato juice

Salt and pepper

1 cup olive oil

1 tablespoon sugar

In a large bowl, combine the tomatoes, onion, garlic, marjoram, vinegar, cumin, coriander, curry powder, paprika, and tomato juice. Cover and let marinate for 3 hours. Whisk in the oil and sugar and then blend in a food processor until smooth. Chill for 4 hours before serving.

Yield: 8 servings

—Chef Brad Parsons

Per serving: 318 Cal.; 49 GI; 3g Prot.; 17g Carb.; 4g SFA; 20g MUFA; 3g PUFA; 0.2g Omega-3; 65mg Calc.; 260mg Sod.; 785mg Pot.; 2mg Iron; 0.1mg Phytoestrogen; 4g Fiber

The "good" cholesterol

HDL is considered the "good" cholesterol because it protects you from having a heart attack. It's different from the other cholesterol levels; the higher your HDL, the better. Several things can help you increase your HDL level: Quit smoking, lose excess weight, eat a good diet, and exercise. It's simple—healthy lifestyle changes can increase your HDL and decrease your risk of heart attack.

borscht (beet soup)

If you're hot, eat it cold. If you're cold, eat it hot. Either way it's delicious, either before a meal or with a salad for a refreshing light meal on its own. Beets are a great source of fiber, vitamin C, magnesium, potassium, folate, and manganese.

Place the cabbage, potatoes, celery, onion, and bell pepper in a large, heavy saucepan. Add the water and salt and bring to a boil over high heat. Reduce the heat to medium and cook for about 45 minutes, or until the vegetables are tender.

Meanwhile, heat the canola oil in a medium saucepan over medium-high heat. Add the beets and carrots and sauté briefly. Reduce the heat to medium, add enough water to cover, and cook for 20 minutes. Add the tomato sauce, mix well, and add this mixture to the cabbage mixture and stir well to combine. Continue to cook over medium heat for 50 minutes longer. Add the garlic to the borsch and cook for 5 more minutes. Allow to cool to room temperature, and then place in a large container and refrigerate. Serve cold to cool hot flashes. Garnish each serving with 1 tablespoon of fat-free sour cream.

Yield: 10 servings

——*Dr. Mache's Kitchen*

Per serving: 61 Cal.; 58 GI; 2g Prot.; 14g Carb.; 0g SFA; 0g MUFA; 0g PUFA; 0g Omega-3; 52mg Calc.; 180mg Sod.; 458mg Pot.; 1mg Iron; 0mg Phytoestrogen; 4g Fiber

1 small head of green cabbage, shredded

2 potatoes, cut into 1- to 2-inch cubes

4 medium ribs of celery, diced

1 onion, diced

1 red or green bell pepper, seeded and diced

5 quarts water

½ teaspoon salt

1 teaspoon canola oil

4 beets, trimmed, peeled, and shredded

2 carrots, shredded

1 (15-ounce) can tomato sauce

5 to 6 cloves of garlic, minced

Fat-free sour cream for garnish

mushroom-barley soup

 This meatless adaptation of the classic soup tastes wonderful and is so healthy. Serve it with a green salad with celery, walnuts, and feta cheese, and a loaf of warm sourdough bread.

2/3 cup pearl barley (use quick-cooking barley or soak barley in water overnight to cut cooking time)

8 cups reduced-sodium chicken or vegetable broth

2 tablespoons olive oil

1 yellow onion, chopped

1 teaspoon minced garlic (about 2 cloves)

2½ to 3 cups sliced mushrooms

2 ribs of celery, thinly sliced

3 carrots, peeled and thinly sliced

1 tablespoon Worcestershire sauce

2 tablespoons dry sherry (or 1 tablespoon balsamic vinegar) (optional)

¼ teaspoon salt, or to taste

1/8 teaspoon pepper, or to taste

Rinse the barley in cold water (or drain the pre-soaked barley). Combine the broth and barley in a large saucepan and bring it to a boil. Reduce the heat and simmer, covered, stirring occasionally, until it is almost tender. (Note: If you are using quick-cooking barley, it should be tender after 10 minutes; pre-soaked barley should be tender after 20 minutes. If you haven't pre-soaked the barley, then simmer it for 40 minutes.)

Meanwhile, in a large heavy skillet heat the olive oil over medium-high heat. Add the onion and sauté until lightly browned, about 5 minutes. Add the garlic, mushrooms, and celery and sauté until the mushrooms are tender and have turned dark, about 5 more minutes.

After the barley has simmered for 10 to 40 minutes (see note above), add the mushroom-onion mixture, carrots, and Worcestershire sauce to the barley. Simmer, covered, for 10 to 15 minutes, until the barley and carrots are tender. Stir in the sherry (optional, but highly recommended) and warm the soup through. Season the soup with salt and pepper to taste and serve immediately or freeze it for up to 3 months.

Variation: Use the optional sherry and serve the soup with a hot pepper sauce, such as Tabasco.

Side dish salad suggestion: To make the salad, combine
6 cups of chopped iceberg or other lettuce; 2 ribs of celery,
sliced; 2 tablespoons of chopped walnuts; and 2 tablespoons
of crumbled feta cheese. Toss the salad with 2 to 4 tablespoons
of a dressing, such as homemade Maple-Dijon Dressing. (To
make Maple-Dijon Dressing, whisk together ¼ cup of olive oil,
1/8 cup of red wine vinegar, 1 tablespoon of pure maple syrup,
1 teaspoon of Dijon mustard, and ½ teaspoon of herbes de
Provence or dried thyme.)

Side dish bread suggestion: Warm a loaf of sourdough bread
in a 300°F oven for 5 minutes.

Soup yield: 6 (2-cup) servings

—Aviva Goldfarb

Per serving: 191 Cal.; 42 GI; 8.5g Prot.; 28g Carb.; 0.7g SFA; 3g MUFA;
0.7g PUFA; 0g Omega-3; 59mg Calc.; 804mg Sod.; 644mg Pot.; 2mg Iron;
0mg Phytoestrogen; 5g Fiber

fish stew

 This is a mouthwatering and succulent Italian fish stew that can be served year round.

1/3 cup extra-virgin olive oil

1 onion, chopped

6 cloves of garlic, thinly sliced

1 rib of celery, chopped

1 carrot, peeled and chopped

1 (28-ounce) can tomatoes, chopped

1 cup dry white wine

½ pound cod, cut into bite-sized pieces

½ pound snapper, cut into bite-sized pieces

½ pound large shrimps, peeled and deveined

1 teaspoon dried oregano

Handful of Italian parsley, chopped

Salt and pepper

Heat the olive oil in a large saucepan over medium heat. Add the onion, garlic, celery, and carrot and sauté for 8 minutes. Add the tomatoes and wine and bring to a boil, then lower the heat and simmer, covered, for 30 minutes. Add the cod and snapper and simmer, covered, for an additional 15 minutes. Then add the shrimp and simmer, covered, for another 5 minutes. Stir in the oregano, parsley, and salt and pepper to taste. If the stew is too thick, add a little water. Serve immediately.

Yield: 4 servings

—*Karen's Cucina*

Per serving: 336 Cal.; 54 GI; 24g Prot.; 15.5g Carb.; 3g SFA; 13g MUFA; 3g PUFA; 0.6g Omega-3; 110mg Calc.; 402mg Sod.; 876mg Pot.; 3mg Iron; 0mg Phytoestrogen; 3g Fiber

vegetable stew

 This has become one of my favorite recipes. It's unbelievably hearty, and served with a side of brown rice or pasta it is a lovely meal, or it can be a side dish for an entrée. It's even better heated up the next day.

Heat the canola oil in a large saucepan over medium heat. Add the onions, carrots, squash, eggplant, zucchini, mushrooms, and beans and cook, stirring occasionally, for about 30 minutes, or until the vegetables are tender. Reduce the heat to low and stir in the tomato sauce and ketchup and cook for 15 minutes. Stir in the garlic and salt and pepper to taste and serve garnished with the Parmesan cheese if desired.

Yield: 4 to 6 servings

—*Dr. Mache's Kitchen*

Per serving: 193 Cal.; 57 GI; 7g Prot.; 30g Carb.; 0.6g SFA; 4g MUFA; 2g PUFA; 0.7g Omega-3; 77mg Calc.; 598mg Sod.; 1,358mg Pot.; 2mg Iron; 0mg Phytoestrogen; 10g Fiber

2 tablespoons canola oil

2 onions, chopped

2 to 3 carrots, sliced

1 summer squash, sliced

1 eggplant, peeled and sliced

1 zucchini, sliced

1 small package of mushrooms, sliced

1 cup green beans, cut into 2-inch pieces

1 (15-ounce) can tomato sauce

1 tablespoon ketchup

3 cloves of garlic, minced

Salt and pepper

Grated Parmesan cheese for garnish (optional)

lentil stew

 This is a very healthy recipe that contains aromatic seasonings and no oils, and it is quick and easy to make. Add a salad for a healthy light meal. Lentils may increase your HDL (or "good" cholesterol).

3 cups water

1 cup lentils, washed and drained

2 large carrots, diced

1 rib of celery, diced

1 (8-ounce) can tomato sauce

½ cup canned chickpeas, drained and rinsed

1 teaspoon ground cumin

½ teaspoon ground coriander

½ teaspoon snipped dill

Pour the water into a medium-sized saucepan and add the lentils. Bring to a boil over high heat and add all the other ingredients. Reduce the heat and simmer, covered, stirring occasionally, for about 40 minutes, or until the lentils are tender.

Yield: 4 servings

—Dr. Mache's Kitchen

Per serving: 423 Cal.; 25 GI; 26g Prot.; 64g Carb.; 1g SFA; 2g MUFA; 5g PUFA; 0.5g Omega-3; 104mg Calc.; 1,770mg Sod.; 1,332mg Pot.; 9mg Iron; 0mg Phytoestrogen; 18g Fiber

Salads

watermelon and watercress salad

This light and healthy salad is great to serve for lunch. To save time, you can make the dressing ahead of time. This is a perfect addition to a summer barbeque or light luncheon. No matter how you slice it, watermelon is great for you. It's packed with antioxidants and it's an excellent source of vitamins A, B, and E. Watermelon is also rich in electrolytes, sodium, and potassium, which we lose when we perspire during those hot flashes.

VINAIGRETTE:

2 shallots

½ cup orange juice

½ cup rice wine vinegar

2 teaspoons salt

1½ cups canola oil

¼ cup sesame oil

SALAD:

4 bunches of watercress

4 cups watermelon, large dice

¼ cup pecans, toasted

To make the vinaigrette, put the shallots, orange juice, vinegar, and salt in a food processor and purée until smooth. Combine the canola and sesame oils in a mixing bowl and pour in a steady stream into the processor while running. When the vinaigrette is thoroughly blended, pour it into a cruet and refrigerate.

To make the salad, wash the watercress well and remove any large stems. Combine the watercress and watermelon in a mixing bowl and toss with ½ cup of the vinaigrette. (The remaining vinaigrette can be refrigerated and used for another salad.) To serve, arrange the salad pleasingly on serving plates and sprinkle with the toasted pecans.

Yield: 4 to 6 servings

—*Chef Tres Hundertmark*

Per serving: 482 Cal.; 63 GI; 1g Prot.; 9g Carb.; 4g SFA; 30g MUFA; 15g PUFA; 4g Omega-3; 14mg Calc.; 605mg Sod.; 161mg Pot.; 0.4mg Iron; 0mg Phytoestrogen; 1g Fiber

Power produce
Use fruits and/or vegetables to replace some of the other foods you're eating to unleash their power and reduce calories in your diet.

dungeness crab salad with peas, thai basil, greens, mint, and meyer lemon vinaigrette

 Dungeness crab is the best crab on earth, and this delectable salad, made with the freshest of ingredients, is truly refreshing.

To make the vinaigrette, put the lemon juice and sugar in a saucepan and bring to a gentle boil over medium-high heat. Cook, uncovered, until the sauce has reduced by half. (You will have more vinaigrette than you need for this recipe.)

To make the lemon vinaigrette, you will need to balance it by taste because the acidity of the lemons will vary the amount of lemon juice and vinegar you will need. Combine the lemon syrup, oil, and lemon juice in a mixing bowl. Add the vinegar to taste and balance with more oil if necessary. Set aside.

To make the basil oil, blanch the basil in boiling salted water for 20 seconds and then shock it in ice water. Wring out the water and place in a food processor. Add the oil and purée. Add a touch of salt and put the purée in a stainless saucepan and bring to a boil over medium-high heat. Turn off the heat, cover, and allow to steep for 15 minutes. Strain the oil through cheesecloth or a chinois strainer. Put the strained oil into a squirt bottle and set aside.

To make the salad, in a mixing bowl, combine the crabmeat, peas, mint, and basil and season to taste with the vinaigrette. Season with salt and pepper and form into a ring mold. Pack down and remove the ring. Garnish with the micro greens. Serve with the lemon vinaigrette and basil oil on the side.

Yield: 4 servings

—*Chef Neal Fraser*

Per serving: 765 Cal.; 59 GI; 13g Prot.; 73g Carb.; 5g SFA; 8g MUFA; 34g PUFA; 0.4g Omega-3; 126mg Calc.; 475mg Sod.; 440mg Pot.; 2mg Iron; 0mg Phytoestrogen; 2g Fiber

VINAIGRETTE:

1 cup Meyer lemon juice

1 cup sugar

LEMON VINAIGRETTE:

½ cup lemon syrup

½ cup grape seed oil

Juice of 2 Meyer lemons

Rice wine vinegar

BASIL OIL:

¾ cup chopped basil

6 tablespoons grape seed oil

Salt

SALAD:

½ pound Dungeness crabmeat

1/3 cup frozen green peas, thawed

1 tablespoon julienned mint

1 tablespoon julienned Thai basil

¾ cup mixed micro greens

Salt and pepper

Ring mold to form the crab salad

asian tuna salad

 This is a delicious tuna salad with an Asian twist. A must-try!

MARINADE:

3 tablespoons low-sodium soy sauce

½ teaspoon wasabi paste

1 tablespoon sake

1 (7-ounce) piece of fresh tuna

DRESSING:

4 tablespoons low-sodium soy sauce

2 tablespoons lime juice

3 teaspoons sesame oil

2 teaspoons brown sugar

SALAD:

1 tablespoon sesame oil

1 cup torn field greens

4 grape tomatoes, halved

¼ cucumber, peeled and sliced

To make the marinade, combine the soy sauce, wasabi paste, and sake in a mixing bowl and mix well.

Place the tuna in a shallow dish and cover with the marinade. Cover and place in the refrigerator and marinate for 4 hours.

Meanwhile, to make the dressing, whisk together the soy sauce, lime juice, oil, and brown sugar and set aside.

To make the salad, heat the oil in a small skillet over high heat and sear each side of the tuna (no more than 20 seconds on each side). Arrange the greens, tomatoes, and cucumber on a salad plate and break up the seared tuna and arrange on top of the salad. Drizzle with the dressing and serve.

Yield: 2 servings

—*Chef Jeffrey S. Merry*

Per serving: 150 Cal.; 52 GI; 15g Prot.; 14g Carb.; 1g SFA; 1g MUFA; 1g PUFA; 0.6g Omega-3; 47mg Calc.; 1,912mg Sod.; 609mg Pot.; 2mg Iron; 1mg Phytoestrogen; 2g Fiber

summer salad

The complementary ingredients in this salad will surely soothe your taste buds. This is a great recipe—nice and refreshing. Add some grilled or Cajun chicken, and this salad is awesome!

Combine the greens, nuts, cranberries, cheese, apple, and strawberries in a mixing bowl. Add the raspberry vinaigrette and salt and pepper to taste and toss. Serve on 4 individual plates with a wedge of lemon for each diner. Enjoy!

Yield: 4 servings

—John Liberatore

Per serving: 420 Cal.; 50 GI; 14g Prot.; 32g Carb.; 6g SFA; 9g MUFA; 12g PUFA; 2g Omega-3; 291mg Calc.; 217mg Sod.; 452mg Pot.; 2mg Iron; 0mg Phytoestrogen; 6g Fiber

6 large handfuls of torn mixed field greens

¼ cup walnuts (or almonds), candied and/or roasted

¼ cup sun-dried cranberries

4 ounces mozzarella cheese, diced

1 Granny Smith apple, cored and sliced

8 to 10 strawberries, sliced

¼ cup raspberry vinaigrette

Salt and pepper

1 small lemon, quartered

arugula and tomato salad

 Arugula is rich in many essential vitamins and minerals, as well as important phytochemicals. Arugula is popular in Italy and has a spicy little leaf with a peppery taste. This recipe is low in calories but high in vitamins.

1/3 cup extra-virgin olive oil

4 tablespoons lemon juice

1 tablespoon lemon zest

1 clove of garlic, minced

¾ teaspoon sugar

Salt and pepper

8 cups arugula, washed and dried

1 tomato, cut into thin wedges

In a small bowl, combine the oil, lemon juice, lemon zest, garlic, sugar, and salt and pepper to taste and whisk until blended. Set aside.

Place the arugula in a salad bowl and toss with the dressing. Arrange the tomato wedges on top and serve immediately.

Yield: 4 servings

—*Karen's Cucina*

Per serving: 181 Cal.; 48 GI; 1g Prot.; 4g Carb.; 2g SFA; 13g MUFA; 2g PUFA; 0.2g Omega-3; 72mg Calc.; 16mg Sod.; 242mg Pot.; 1mg Iron; 0mg Phytoestrogen; 1g Fiber

spinach salad with feta and prosciutto

 You will receive great raves after serving this salad.

Wash and dry the spinach and place in a salad bowl. In a small skillet, heat the olive oil over medium-high heat. Add the garlic and sauté for about 3 minutes, until golden brown. Reduce the heat to low and add the pine nuts, prosciutto, and salt and pepper to taste and cook for an additional 5 minutes. Add to the spinach with the feta cheese and toss. Serve immediately.

Yield: 4 servings

—Karen's Cucina

Per serving: 261 Cal.; 37 GI; 8g Prot.; 5g Carb.; 5g SFA; 12g MUFA; 4g PUFA; 0.3g Omega-3; 180mg Calc.; 403mg Sod.; 574mg Pot.; 3mg Iron; 0mg Phytoestrogen; 2g Fiber

¾ pound baby spinach

¼ cup extra-virgin olive oil

1 clove of garlic, diced

¼ cup toasted pine nuts

¼ cup diced prosciutto

Salt and pepper

½ cup crumbled feta cheese

tuna and bean salad

 This recipe includes the fiber benefits of the cannelloni beans, and the spinach is a great antioxidant as well as being high in fiber. With this great combination of ingredients, you'll get requests for this recipe.

2 (7-ounce) cans Italian tuna

2 cups canned cannelloni beans, drained and rinsed

¼ cup red onion, diced

6 tablespoons capers, drained

½ cup celery, diced

1 Roma tomato, diced

3 tablespoons lemon juice

6 tablespoons extra-virgin olive oil

Salt and pepper

Combine the tuna, beans, onions, capers, celery, and tomato in a large bowl. Whisk together the lemon juice, olive oil, and salt and pepper to taste and toss with the tuna mixture. Serve immediately.

Yield: 4 servings

—*Karen's Cucina*

Per serving: 147 Cal.; 51 GI; 26g Prot.; 7g Carb.; 0.2g SFA; 0.1g MUFA; 0.4g PUFA; 0.3g Omega-3; 48mg Calc.; 933mg Sod.; 420mg Pot.; 2.5mg Iron; 0mg Phytoestrogen; 3g Fiber

watercress salad with fennel

 This recipe is rich in phytoestrogens and fiber. It is very different, very fresh, and very good!

Wash, dry, and trim the fennel, removing any blemished leaves. Cut each head of fennel in half and slice as thinly as possible and place in a large salad bowl.

Rinse and dry the watercress and cut off any tough stems. Add to the salad bowl with the fennel.

In a small bowl, combine the olive oil, vinegar, capers, sugar, and salt and pepper to taste and mix well. Pour over the fennel and watercress and toss lightly. Serve immediately.

Yield: 4 servings

—*Karen's Cucina*

Per serving: 158 Cal., 67 GI; 1.5g Prot.; 9g Carb.; 2g SFA; 10g MUFA;
2g PUFA; 0.1g Omega-3; 60mg Calc.; 189mg Sod.; 490mg Pot.; 1mg Iron;
0mg Phytoestrogen; 4g Fiber

2 large heads of fennel

1 bunch of watercress

¼ cup extra-virgin olive oil

1 tablespoon white wine vinegar

2 tablespoons capers, drained

¼ teaspoon sugar

Salt and pepper

tortellini and olive salad

 This tortellini salad is good, quick, and easy to make. It's a hit at luncheons and potluck dinners, and it can be served either cold or hot.

¾ pound tortellini pasta

½ cup sun-dried tomatoes, diced

½ cup chopped spinach

½ cup sliced pitted black olives

¼ cup freshly grated Parmesan cheese

Juice of 1 lemon

¼ cup extra-virgin olive oil

3 cloves of garlic, minced

Salt and pepper

Cook the pasta al dente, according to the package instructions. Drain and transfer to a salad bowl. Add the spinach, olives, sun-dried tomatoes, and Parmesan cheese to the pasta. In a small bowl, whisk together the lemon juice, olive oil, and garlic and toss with the pasta mixture. Season with salt and pepper to taste and serve immediately.

Yield: 4 servings

—*Karen's Cucina*

Per serving: 372 Cal.; 62 GI; 13g Prot.; 23g Carb.; 7g SFA; 14g MUFA; 2g PUFA; 0.2g Omega-3; 268mg Calc.; 576mg Sod.; 353mg Pot.; 3mg Iron; 0mg Phytoestrogen; 2g Fiber

roasted beet and asparagus salad

 This recipe is a wonderful way to blend together the health benefits of beets and asparagus. Spruce up any meal, including holiday meals, with this unique salad.

Preheat the oven to 400°F.

Wrap the beets in aluminum foil and place on a rack in the oven. Roast for 1 hour, or until they can easily be pierced with a knife. Remove from the oven and let cool. When cool, peel and slice and set aside.

Steam the asparagus for about 5 minutes, until tender, and then plunge into ice cold water to stop cooking. Drain and set aside.

In small bowl, whisk the oil, vinegar, and salt and pepper to taste. Place the lettuce on a serving platter and arrange the asparagus spears and beets on top. Pour the dressing over top and serve immediately.

Yield: 4 servings

—*Karen's Cucina*

Per serving: 450 Cal.; 59 GI; 5g Prot.; 18g Carb.; 5g SFA; 29g MUFA; 4g PUFA; 0.3g Omega-3; 74mg Calc.; 107mg Sod.; 720mg Pot.; 4mg Iron; 0.06mg Phytoestrogen; 6g Fiber

5 small beets, washed and trimmed

1 pound thin asparagus, ends trimmed

¾ cup extra-virgin olive oil

¼ cup balsamic vinegar

Salt and pepper

8 cups torn lettuce

> ### Let off some steam!
> Steamed vegetables are delicious and low in calories. Steam until the color is bright and try not to overcook them.

caprese salad

Caprese salad—it's colorful, refreshing, and delicious. This tomato and mozzarella salad is especially good on very hot days. Serve with some crusty bread with extra-virgin olive oil for dipping.

2 medium vine-ripe tomatoes, sliced

7 ounces part-skim, low-sodium mozzarella, thinly sliced

5 tablespoons chopped basil

2 tablespoons extra-virgin olive oil

1 tablespoon lemon juice

Salt and pepper

On a serving platter, arrange the tomatoes and cheese in overlapping rows and sprinkle the basil over top.

Whisk together the olive oil, lemon juice, and salt and pepper to taste and drizzle over the tomatoes and cheese and serve immediately.

Yield: 4 servings

—*Karen's Cucina*

Per serving: 285 Cal.; 40 GI; 16g Prot.; 5g Carb.; 7g SFA; 7g MUFA; 1g PUFA; 0.1g Omega-3; 524mg Calc.; 377mg Sod.; 213mg Pot.; 0.3mg Iron; 0mg Phytoestrogen; 1g Fiber

salade niçoise

This fabulous salad celebrates the veggies of the season and pairs them with tuna. Talk about good food that's good for you!

To make the dressing, in a small bowl combine the lemon juice, sugar, anchovy paste, mustard, shallots, and pepper. Slowly whisk in the olive oil.

Put the potatoes in a small saucepan and cover with water. Bring to a boil over high heat. Once boiling, reduce the heat and simmer until the potatoes are tender, approximately 10 minutes. Drain, halve, and set aside.

Fill a saucepan with 2 inches of water and bring to a boil over high heat. Add the beans and bring to a boil again. Reduce the heat and simmer for about 8 minutes, just until they are tender. Drain and set aside.

Place the lettuce leaves in a serving bowl and drizzle with half the dressing. Arrange the tuna, eggs, olives, potatoes, cherry tomatoes, and tomato slices decoratively over the lettuce. Drizzle with the remaining dressing and serve immediately.

Yield: 4 servings

—*Karen's Cucina*

Per serving: 316 Cal.; 48 GI; 18g Prot.; 16g Carb.; 3.5g SFA; 14g MUFA; 3g PUFA; 0.3g Omega-3; 99mg Calc.; 1,004mg Sod.; 818mg Pot.; 3mg Iron; 0mg Phytoestrogen; 5.5g Fiber

DRESSING:

2 tablespoons lemon juice

Pinch of sugar

2 teaspoons anchovy paste

1 teaspoon Dijon mustard

2 tablespoons minced shallots

Pinch of pepper

¼ cup extra-virgin olive oil

SALAD:

4 small new potatoes, unpeeled

½ pound green beans, trimmed

1 head of tender baby lettuce, leaves separated

1 (7-ounce) can solid white tuna, drained and flaked

2 hard-boiled eggs, quartered lengthwise

¾ cup Niçoise olives, pitted

15 cherry tomatoes

1 pound tomatoes, cut into ¼-inch slices

celery and walnut salad

This cool-weather salad is very simple and surprisingly delicious. Enjoy the great mix of sweet and crunchy ingredients!

6 ribs of celery, cut into 1/8-inch slices

1 cup walnuts, toasted

20 pitted black olives

2 ounces Parmigiano-Reggiano cheese, cut into ¼-inch pieces

6 tablespoons extra-virgin olive oil

1 tablespoon red wine vinegar

½ teaspoon dried oregano

Salt and pepper

Combine the celery, walnuts, olives, and cheese in a salad bowl. In a small bowl, whisk the olive oil, vinegar, and oregano and toss with the celery mixture, adding salt and pepper to taste. Serve immediately.

Yield: 4 servings

—*Karen's Cucina*

Per serving: 433 Cal.; 32 GI; 9g Prot.; 7g Carb.; 6g SFA; 19g MUFA; 14g PUFA; 2.5g Omega-3; 238mg Calc.; 451mg Sod.; 289mg Pot.; 2mg Iron; 0mg Phytoestrogen; 3g Fiber

roasted beet salad with grapefruit and chive vinaigrette

 The unique combination of delicious ingredients gives this salad a fantastic flavor. Use locally grown heirloom beets when available.

To make the vinaigrette, put the egg, vinegar, and chives in a food processor and blend until well mixed. Combine the oils, and then slowly add them to the food processor. Blend until the mixture begins to emulsify and turn pale green. If the mixture gets too thick, add the water. Season with salt to taste and set aside.

To make the salad, preheat the oven to 400°F. Lightly toss the beets in the olive oil and salt to taste and place on a baking sheet. Cover with foil and bake for 1 hour, or until tender. Let cool and then peel and cut the beets into a large dice.

On a large plate, arrange the mixed greens, beets, grapefruit segments, and fennel. Finish with the chive vinaigrette and season with salt and pepper to taste. Serve immediately.

Yield: 4 servings

—*Donnie Ferneau Jr., C.E.C.*

Per serving: 638 Cal.; 43 GI; 6g Prot.; 31g Carb.; 5g SFA; 30g MUFA; 18g PUFA; 10g Omega-3; 108mg Calc.; 155mg Sod.; 1,063mg Pot.; 2mg Iron; 0.1mg Phytoestrogen; 8g Fiber

VINAIGRETTE:

1 egg

¼ cup white wine vinegar

½ cup chopped chives

¼ cup flaxseed oil

½ cup canola oil

¼ cup water (if needed)

Salt

SALAD:

1 pound beets, trimmed

¼ cup olive oil

Salt

4 cups (½ pound) organic mixed greens (spinach or arugala will also work)

2 large grapefruits, segmented

1 bulb of fennel, shaved or sliced very thin

Salt and pepper

shepherd's salad

This salad evolved as a celebration of the incredible spring greens received from Your Kitchen Garden Farm in Canby, Oregon, and it appears on the menu at Nostrana in Portland every spring. Its vivid colors are best showcased on a white platter or white serving plates. Every year its return is greeted with orders by the entire staff as well as the customers at the restaurant. There can't be a more healthful, fresh, and taste-rewarding salad for lunch or dinner.

PICKLED RED ONIONS:

2 medium red onions

½ cup water

½ cup apple cider vinegar

1½ tablespoons sugar

3 tablespoons olive oil

1½ teaspoons salt

Generous pinch of pepper

SALAD:

6 cups assorted greens, varying in color, texture, and taste (The restaurant uses mizuna, arugula, rustic arugula, mâche, and chrysanthemum leaf)

1 farm-fresh egg

1 large shallot, minced

2 tablespoons sherry vinegar

Salt

6 to 8 tablespoons walnut oil

½ cup creamy, fresh goat cheese

To make the pickled red onions, peel the onions, leaving the stem-ends intact; cut into sixths (or eighths, if large). In a medium non-reactive saucepan, combine the onions, water, vinegar, sugar, olive oil, salt, and pepper. Bring to a boil and cook, stirring often, for 5 minutes. Remove from the heat and let the onions cool in the liquid.

To make the salad, wash the greens, dry well, and chill.

Hard-boil the egg (see tip below). Set aside.

Squeeze the shallots in a clean kitchen towel to remove any bitter juices. Place in a small mixing bowl. Add the vinegar and salt to taste. Stir well and let sit for 30 minutes (the shallot will soften in bitterness).

Slowly whisk the walnut oil into the vinegar mixture to emulsify, and then season with salt and pepper to taste.

Preheat the oven or toaster oven broiler.

Lightly spread about 2 tablespoons of the goat cheese over each of the ciabatta slices and place under the broiler until golden.

Toss the greens and the walnuts together with enough dressing to coat well, but do not drown them. Arrange on a white platter or on individual plates. Top with the pickled onion and egg quarters, sprinkle with sea salt and a few grindings of pepper, and serve immediately with the bread and cheese.

Yield: 4 servings

—*Chef Cathy Whims*

Tip: To hard-boil the egg, first, use a real farm-fresh egg. Place the egg in a saucepan and cover with cold water. Bring to a boil, and then immediately remove from the heat and cover the saucepan. Set a timer for 7 minutes. When the timer sounds, immediately drain the egg and run cold water over it until it is cool. Peel and quarter lengthwise.

Per serving: 432 Cal.; 60 GI; 12g Prot.; 43g Carb.; 4g SFA; 5g MUFA; 13g PUFA; 2g Omega-3; 91mg Calc.; 1,272mg Sod.; 346mg Pot.; 4mg Iron; 0mg Phytoestrogen; 3g Fiber

4 slices of rustic bread, preferably ciabatta

Walnuts, as local as possible, or, if not, lightly toasted

½ cup pickled red onions (above)

Fleur de Sel sea salt (or Maldon sea salt) (The restaurant uses Flor de Sal, Portuguese sea salt)

Freshly ground pepper

canlis salad

This salad has been on the Canlis menu in Seattle, in a myriad of versions, since 1950. Chef Jason Franey is the current Canlis executive chef and his preparation incorporates the same ingredients as the original. This recipe is for one salad serving; you can increase the salad ingredients by eight to serve eight.

SEASONED CROUTONS:
(Makes about 4 cups to serve 8)

¼ cup butter (½ stick)

1 tablespoon salt

1 tablespoon dried oregano

1 tablespoon Italian seasoning

1 teaspoon freshly ground pepper

1 teaspoon garlic powder

4 cups European-style white bread, cut into ¼-inch cubes

DRESSING:
(Makes about 1 cup to serve 8)

1 coddled egg

¼ cup freshly squeezed lemon juice

1 teaspoon freshly ground pepper

½ cup olive oil

To make the croutons, preheat the oven to 300°F.

Melt the butter over medium heat in a small skillet. Add the salt, oregano, Italian seasoning, pepper, and garlic powder.

Place the bread cubes in a baking dish, add the melted butter mixture and toss to mix well. Bake, stirring every 5 minutes, for 30 to 40 minutes, or until crisp and golden brown. Cool completely at room temperature before serving or storing. (Extra croutons keep in an airtight container at room temperature for several days.)

To make the dressing, in a small bowl, beat the egg with the lemon juice and pepper. Still beating, stream in the olive oil and continue beating for a few seconds to create a smooth dressing. Set aside.

To make the salad, in a large, well-seasoned wooden salad bowl, combine the lettuce, tomatoes, ½ cup of the croutons, the green onion, bacon, oregano, half the cheese, half the mint, and a generous sprinkling of kosher salt and freshly ground pepper. Toss the salad dry to distribute the ingredients evenly, then pour on 2 tablespoons of the dressing and toss again.

Transfer the salad to a serving plate. Finish with the remaining cheese and mint and a generous grinding of pepper.

Yield: 1 serving

—Chef Jason Franey

Per serving (salad): 170 Cal.; 47 GI; 12g Prot.; 10g Carb.; 5g SFA; 3g MUFA; 1g PUFA; 0.3 g Omega-3; 316mg Calc.; 457mg Sod.; 640mg Pot.; 3mg Iron; 0mg Phytoestrogen; 5g Fiber

Per serving (dressing): 132 Cal.; 33 GI; 1g Prot.; 1g Carb.; 2g SFA; 10g MUFA; 1g PUFA; 0.1g Omega-3; 6mg Calc.; 9mg Sod.; 22mg Pot.; 0mg Iron; 0mg Phytoestrogen; 0g Fiber

Per serving (croutons): 105 Cal.; 60 GI; 2g Prot.; 10g Carb.; 3g SFA; 1g MUFA; 0.3g PUFA; 0.05g Omega-3; 291mg Calc.; 450mg Sod.; 44mg Pot.; 1mg Iron; 0mg Phytoestrogen; 1g Fiber

SALAD:

¼ head of romaine lettuce, washed and cut into 1-inch pieces

Heirloom cherry tomatoes, halved or quartered

½ cup croutons (above)

2 tablespoons chopped green onion

2 tablespoons well-done chopped bacon, drained

1 teaspoon dried oregano

3 tablespoons freshly grated Romano cheese, divided

2 tablespoons (or to taste) finely chopped mint, divided

Kosher salt and freshly ground pepper

2 tablespoons dressing (or to taste) (above)

kale with tofu

The key to this recipe is using fresh kale chopped finely so it cooks in less time. This is a delicious and fast way to include a nutritious green leafy vegetable, rich in calcium and vitamins, along with the benefits of soy. Each cup of cooked kale provides 94 milligrams of calcium, 296 milligrams of potassium, 9,620 IU of vitamin A, 17.3 micrograms of folic acid, 53.3 milligrams of vitamin C, and 23.4 milligrams of magnesium, among others.

2 tablespoons olive oil

3 cups finely chopped kale

½ pound tofu, cubed

2 to 3 cloves of garlic, finely chopped

Salt and other seasonings

Heat the olive oil in a skillet over medium-high heat. Add the kale, tofu, and garlic and sauté until the kale is deep green and tender. Remove from the heat and season to taste with salt and your choice of other seasonings. Serve over pasta, brown rice, or alone.

Yield: 4 servings

—*Hari Kaur Khalsa*

Per serving: 193 Cal.; 44 GI; 7g Prot.; 6g Carb.; 1g SFA; 7g MUFA; 1g PUFA; 0.1g Omega-3; 171mg Calc.; 27mg Sod.; 307mg Pot.; 2mg Iron; 13mg Phytoestrogen; 1g Fiber

yogi no-egg egg salad

This recipe is a healthy solution for when you have a craving for egg salad but want to avoid the cholesterol. It's quick and easy to make. Soy has so many nutritional and medicinal benefits that it is now considered a staple for women in perimenopause and menopause.

Mash the tofu with a fork in a large bowl until it becomes crumbly. Add the celery, onion, mayonnaise, mustard, and other seasonings you enjoy; mix thoroughly. Serve on whole-grain or pita bread with sliced tomatoes and sprouts.

Yield: 4 servings

—*Hari Kaur Khalsa*

Per serving: 126 Cal.; 44 GI; 10g Prot.; 4.5g Carb.; 1g SFA; 2g MUFA; 4g PUFA; 0.3g Omega-3; 242mg Calc.; 186mg Sod.; 249mg Pot.; 2mg Iron; 31mg Phytoestrogen; 2g Fiber

1 pound firm low-fat tofu

1 large rib of celery, chopped

¼ cup finely chopped onion

¼ cup tofu mayonnaise (available in health food stores)

1 tablespoon prepared mustard

Seasonings

yogi sesame-yogurt dressing

 When eating raw vegetables, it's great to have a healthy dressing to go with them. According to the yogis, this dressing helps prevent gas, which some people get from eating raw vegetables. This dressing is not only healthy, it is also delicious!

4 sprigs of parsley, chopped

1 rib of celery, chopped

¼ small onion

½ cup sesame seeds

1 clove of garlic, sliced

1 cup plain yogurt

½ cup raw sesame oil

2 tablespoons lemon juice

2 tablespoons soy sauce

1 tablespoon balsamic vinegar

1 teaspoon honey

¼ teaspoon salt

¼ teaspoon pepper

Blend all the ingredients in a food processor on low speed until smooth and serve with a selection of raw vegetables.

Yield: 3 cups

—*Hari Kaur Khalsa*

Per serving: 74 Cal.; 49 GI; 2g Prot.; 3g Carb.; 1g SFA; 2g MUFA; 2g PUFA; 0.02g Omega-3; 34mg Calc.; 165mg Sod.; 71mg Pot.; 0.3mg Iron; 0.05mg Phytoestrogen; 1g Fiber

Pastas

spaghetti puttanesca

 This is a quick and easy meal to make that is jam-packed with flavors galore. In Italy, the word *puttanesca* has a naughty hidden meaning.

¾ pound spaghetti

8 tablespoons extra-virgin olive oil

4 cloves of garlic, chopped

1 (4-ounce) can anchovies

Pinch of red pepper flakes

1 (28-ounce) can diced Italian plum tomatoes

50 pitted Italian black olives

5 tablespoons capers, drained and rinsed

Handful of chopped parsley

Salt and pepper

Cook the spaghetti al dente according to the package instructions. (I prefer the Barilla brand.) Drain and set aside.

Heat the olive oil in a large skillet over medium heat, and then add the garlic, anchovies, and red pepper flakes and sauté for 3 to 4 minutes. Add the tomatoes and cook for 10 minutes longer, and then add the olives and capers and cook for 5 additional minutes. Add the cooked spaghetti and mix well with the sauce. Stir in the parsley and salt and pepper to taste and serve immediately.

Yield: 4 servings

—*Karen's Cucina*

Per serving: 659 Cal.; 43 GI; 18g Prot.; 76g Carb.; 5g SFA; 24g MUFA; 4g PUFA; 0.5g Omega-3; 178mg Calc.; 1,460mg Sod.; 566mg Pot.; 7mg Iron; 0mg Phytoestrogen; 10g Fiber

tuscan-style penne with white beans and grilled chicken and basil

 This pasta dish is an excellent dinner choice. Made with fresh escarole and cooked in broth with sautéed garlic and seasoned chicken, it is super-tasty!

Heat the oil in a large skillet over medium heat. Add the garlic and sauté until tender but not browned. Add the escarole, beans, chicken, and chicken broth and bring to a simmer, and then add the cooked pasta and cook until heated through. Transfer to individual bowls and sprinkle with the basil.

Yield: 4 servings

—*Chef Jeffrey S. Merry*

Per serving: 258 Cal.; 42 GI; 18g Prot.; 43g Carb.; 0.5g SFA; 0.6g MUFA; 0.6g PUFA; 0g Omega-3; 53mg Calc.; 117mg Sod.; 294mg Pot.; 2mg Iron; 0mg Phytoestrogen; 6g Fiber

1 tablespoon olive oil

1 teaspoon chopped garlic

2½ cups coarsely chopped escarole

½ cup canned white cannelloni beans, drained

4 ounces grilled chicken breast, cut into bite-sized pieces

½ cup chicken broth

8 ounces penne rigate pasta, cooked

1 teaspoon chopped basil

lemon fettuccine

This recipe is a show-stopper and can be served at an elaborate meal. The intense lemony flavor with the pasta always makes guests ask for seconds.

¾ pound fresh or dry fettuccine pasta

4 tablespoons extra-virgin olive oil

3 cloves of garlic, chopped

Pinch of red pepper flakes

Juice of 3 lemons

Zest of 3 lemons

1 tablespoon unsalted butter

Salt and pepper

4 tablespoons chopped Italian parsley

¾ cup freshly grated Pecorino-Romano cheese

Cook the fettucine al dente according to the package instructions. Drain and set aside.

Heat the olive oil in a large skillet over medium-low heat. Add the garlic and red pepper flakes and sauté for about 3 minutes, until the garlic is tender but not browned. Add the lemon juice and zest, bring to a boil, and then remove from the heat and add the butter and the salt and pepper to taste. Add the cooked fettuccine and toss well. Stir in the parsley and cheese and serve immediately.

Yield: 4 servings

—*Karen's Cucina*

Per serving: 490 Cal.; 40 GI; 12g Prot.; 51g Carb.; 6g SFA; 14g MUFA; 1g PUFA; 0.2g Omega-3; 122mg Calc.; 101mg Sod.; 160mg Pot.; 3mg Iron; 0.03mg Phytoestrogen; 3g Fiber

To lose or control weight . . .
Replace 1 cup of the rice or pasta in your dish with 1 cup of chopped vegetables, such as tomatoes, squash, onions, peppers, or broccoli.

spaghetti with tuna

There are an infinite number of tuna sauces. This one is quick and easy to make and is surprisingly tasty.

In a large saucepan, cook the spaghetti al dente according to the package instructions. Drain and set aside.

Heat the olive oil in a 12-inch skillet over medium-low heat. Add the garlic and sauté until tender but not browned. Add the anchovies, mashing them with a wooden spoon. Add the tomatoes and stir in the tuna, olives, capers, red pepper flakes, and parsley. Simmer on low heat for 10 minutes. Add the spaghetti, mixing it well with the sauce, and cook for 3 to 4 minutes longer, until it is thoroughly mixed and heated through. Serve immediately.

Yield: 4 servings

—*Karen's Cucina*

Per serving: 532 Cal.; 43 GI; 24g Prot.; 73g Carb.; 3g SFA; 12g MUFA; 3g PUFA; 0.4g Omega-3; 143mg Calc.; 1,168mg Sod.; 604mg Pot.; 6mg Iron; 0mg Phytoestrogen; 9g Fiber

¾ pound spaghetti

¼ cup extra-virgin olive oil

3 cloves of garlic, chopped

1 (4-ounce) can anchovies

1 (28-ounce) can Italian plum tomatoes

1 (3-ounce) can tuna in olive oil, drained and flaked

8 pitted olives, halved

5 tablespoons capers, drained and rinsed

Pinch of red pepper flakes

Handful of chopped Italian parsley

Salt and pepper

lemon-walnut farfalle

 This simple, no-fuss recipe is great. The anchovies and nuts are a great combination.

¾ pound farfalle pasta

2 tablespoons extra-virgin olive oil

6 cloves of garlic, chopped

1 (4-ounce) can anchovies

1 cup finely chopped walnuts

Zest of 1 large lemon

½ cup freshly grated Parmesan cheese

Handful of chopped Italian parsley

Cook the pasta al dente according to the package instructions. When it is almost done, remove 1 cup of the cooking water and set aside. When the pasta is done, drain the rest of the water and set the pasta aside.

Heat the olive oil in large skillet over medium-high heat. Add the garlic and sauté for 2 minutes, until tender but not browned. Reduce the heat to low and add the anchovies, walnuts, and lemon zest and cook for 3 minutes. Stir the cup of cooking water into the sauce, and then add the pasta and mix well. Transfer to a warmed serving bowl and serve immediately sprinkled with the cheese and parsley.

Yield: 4 servings

—*Karen's Cucina*

Per serving: 707 Cal.; 46 GI; 26g Prot.; 78g Carb.; 6g SFA; 9g MUFA; 15g PUFA; 3g Omega-3; 249mg Calc.; 643mg Sod.; 328mg Pot.; 4mg Iron; 0mg Phytoestrogen; 6g Fiber

penne with pine nuts in tomato sauce

 When time's tight, this is one of the most delicious, easiest (and fastest!) solutions.

In a large saucepan, cook the penne al dente according to the package instructions. When it is almost done, remove ¾ cup of the cooking water and set aside. When the pasta is done, drain and set aside.

In a large skillet, toast the pine nuts over medium heat until golden brown. Add the olive oil, garlic, red pepper flakes, and salt to taste and sauté until the garlic is tender but not browned. Add the tomatoes, mashing them with a wooden spoon, parsley, and basil. Bring to a boil, and then reduce the heat and simmer for 20 minutes. Stir the reserved cooking water into the sauce, and then add the pasta and toss to mix well. Serve with the Parmesan cheese sprinkled over top.

Yield: 4 servings

—*Karen's Cucina*

Per serving: 612 Cal.; 42 GI; 19g Prot.; 73g Carb.; 5g SFA; 14g MUFA; 8g PUFA; 0.2g Omega-3; 207mg Calc.; 408mg Sod.; 642mg Pot.; 6mg Iron; 0mg Phytoestrogen; 9.5g Fiber

¾ pound penne pasta

½ cup pine nuts

4 tablespoons extra-virgin olive oil

4 cloves of garlic, chopped

Pinch of red pepper flakes

Salt

1 (28-ounce) can tomatoes

4 tablespoons chopped Italian parsley

Handful of chopped basil

¾ tablespoons unsalted butter

¼ cup freshly grated Parmesan cheese

penne with golden raisins, spinach, and chickpeas

 This is a simple, easy recipe that is always a crowd pleaser.

¾ pound penne pasta

4 tablespoons extra-virgin olive oil

4 cloves of garlic, chopped

1 (19-ounce) can chickpeas, drained and rinsed

12 ounces spinach, washed and dried

½ cup golden raisins

Salt

Pinch of red pepper flakes

¾ cup chicken broth

In a large saucepan, cook the penne al dente according to the package instructions. Drain and set aside.

In a large skillet, heat the olive oil over medium-high heat. Add the garlic and sauté until it is a light golden color. Stir in the chickpeas, spinach, raisins, salt to taste, and the red pepper flakes. Add the chicken broth and simmer over low heat for 20 minutes. Add the pasta and toss to mix well. Serve immediately.

Yield: 4 servings

—*Karen's Cucina*

Per serving: 712 Cal.; 45 GI; 28g Prot.; 116g Carb.; 2.5g SFA; 11g MUFA; 3g PUFA; 0.3g Omega-3; 196mg Calc.; 332mg Sod.; 1,150mg Pot.; 9mg Iron; 2mg Phytoestrogen; 17g Fiber

linguine with seafood

Highly recommended! This is an awesome and delicious dish. The flavor from the seafood really makes this sauce.

Cook the linguine al dente according to the package instructions. Drain and set aside.

Heat the olive oil in a large skillet over low heat. Add the shrimp, scallops, and salt and pepper to taste and cook for 3 minutes. Add the calamari, crabmeat, and garlic and cook an additional 2 minutes. Then add the olives, sun-dried tomatoes, 2 tablespoons of their reserved oil, and the tomatoes and cook for 2 more minutes. Add the linguine and toss to mix well, and then stir in the butter, basil, and salt and pepper to taste. Sprinkle with the parsley and serve immediately.

Yield: 4 servings

—*Karen's Cucina*

Per serving: 688 Cal.; 47 GI; 35g Prot.; 86g Carb.; 4g SFA; 12g MUFA; 3g PUFA; 0.6g Omega-3; 173mg Calc.; 575mg Sod.; 897mg Pot.; 8mg Iron; 0.008mg Phytoestrogen; 7 g Fiber

¾ pound linguine pasta

¼ cup extra-virgin olive oil

25 medium shrimp, peeled and deveined

4 ounces medium scallops

4 ounces calamari

4 ounces fresh crabmeat, flaked

6 cloves of garlic, chopped

¼ cup quartered Kalamata olives

¼ cup sun-dried tomatoes packed in olive oil (reserve the oil)

1 (28-ounce) can tomatoes

1 tablespoon unsalted butter

¼ cup chopped basil leaves

Salt and pepper

¼ cup chopped Italian parsley

vermicelli with clam sauce

 This is a very quick and easy sauce to top vermicelli or any pasta.

¾ pound vermicelli pasta

½ cup extra-virgin olive oil

6 cloves of garlic, thinly sliced

2 (10-ounce) cans chopped clams, with juice

Pinch of red pepper flakes

½ cup sliced olives

Juice of 1 lemon

2 cups dry white wine

1 (28-ounce) can tomatoes

½ cup chopped Italian parsley

Salt and pepper

Cook the pasta al dente according to the package instructions. Drain and set aside.

In a large skillet, heat the olive oil over low heat. Add the garlic, clams and their juice, red pepper flakes, and salt and pepper to taste and cook for 4 minutes. Add the olives, lemon juice, wine, and tomatoes (mashing them with a wooden spoon), and parsley and cook for an additional 10 minutes. Add the cooked pasta and toss to mix well. Serve immediately.

Yield: 4 servings

—*Karen's Cucina*

Tip: The fat calories in this recipe are predominantly (23%) monounsaturated fat; the saturated fat is very low (< 5%). If you want to reduce total fat calories, you can leave out the olives, or reduce the quantity. Also a good source of iron.

Per serving: 871 Cal.; 46 GI; 27g Prot.; 93g Carb.; 5g SFA; 23g MUFA; 4g PUFA; 0.4g Omega-3; 185mg Calc.; 715mg Sod.; 908mg Pot.; 19mg Iron; 0.032mg Phytoestrogen; 8 g Fiber

pan-seared sardines, slow-cooked grains, swiss chard,
golden raisins, pine nuts, and smoked paprika, page 72

soy grilled salmon skewers, page 152

roasted beet salad with grapefruit and chive vinaigrette, page 115

clockwise from top:
moroccan chicken over apricot-cranberry couscous, page 167

tuscan-style penne with white beans and
grilled chicken and basil, page 125

cold tofu with cilantro, green onions, and
soy sesame sauce, page 180

farfalle with tomatoes and goat cheese

 This is an unforgettable, delicious recipe for Italian pasta served vegetarian style. Your guests will ask for seconds.

Cook the pasta al dente according to the package instructions. Drain and set aside.

Heat the olive oil in a large skillet over medium heat. Add the garlic, tomatoes, pine nuts, red pepper flakes, and salt and pepper to taste and cook for 10 minutes, stirring frequently. Then add the basil and cook for an additional 4 minutes. Add the pasta and cheese and toss to mix well. Serve immediately.

Yield: 4 servings

—*Karen's Cucina*

Per serving: 686 Cal.; 47 GI; 21g Prot.; 85g Carb.; 5g SFA; 14g MUFA; 8g PUFA; 0.2g Omega-3; 131mg Calc.; 340mg Sod.; 640mg Pot.; 7mg Iron; 0.032mg Phytoestrogen; 7g Fiber

¾ pound farfalle pasta

4 tablespoons extra-virgin olive oil

8 cloves of garlic, thinly sliced

1 (28-ounce) can diced Italian plum tomatoes

½ cup pine nuts

Pinch of red pepper flakes

Salt and pepper

1 cup torn basil

6 ounces soft goat cheese, crumbled

What's in your stomach?
Make two fists with your hands and hold them in front of your stomach. This is the total amount of food you should have in your stomach at any one time. The yogic prescription for filling your stomach is one-third food, one-third water, and one-third space for digestion.

smashed tomatoes and penne

 This recipe from *Good Carbs, Bad Carbs* author Johanna Burani allows 2½ ounces of pasta per person, which is plenty for a light meal or *i primi* (first course). With pasta, take notice of the cooking times the manufacturer suggests, but ignore the suggested serving size. They are almost always too much pasta for a single meal, sometimes suggesting you use 1 pound of pasta for four people! That's serious carb overload for most.

4 tablespoons extra-virgin olive oil

2 large cloves of garlic, minced

1 pound grape (cherry) tomatoes, washed and halved lengthwise

½ pound penne or other short pasta

1 teaspoon salt

In a medium-sized saucepan, heat 2 tablespoons of the olive oil over medium-low heat for just a minute. Add the garlic and tomatoes and give it all a good stir, then cover the saucepan and let it simmer gently for 10 minutes, stirring occasionally. Remove the pan from the heat and, with the back of a wooden spoon or a fork, lightly smash the tomatoes.

In the meantime, bring a large saucepan of 2 to 3 quarts of water to the boil, add the salt, and cook the pasta for 10 to 11 minutes, until al dente, following the package instructions. Do not overcook. Drain the pasta and add it to the saucepan with the tomatoes and garlic. Drizzle the remaining olive oil over the pasta mixture, stir so it is all well combined, and serve immediately. Top with fresh basil leaves and freshly grated Romano cheese if you wish.

Yield: 4 servings

—The University of Sydney Glycemic Index and GI Database

Per serving: 388 Cal.; 47 GI; 10g Prot.; 48g Carb.; 2g SFA; 10g MUFA; 2g PUFA; 0.1g Omega-3; 25mg Calc.; 228mg Sod.; 344mg Pot.; 2mg Iron; 0mg Phytoestrogen; 4g Fiber

pesto

This is a quick and easy pesto sauce to top any pasta. It makes a great change from red sauce.

Combine the basil, garlic, and nuts in the bowl of a food processor (or half the recipe at a time and use a blender). Pulse a few times and then pour in the olive oil in a steady stream while the motor is running. Shut the motor off and add the cheeses, a pinch of salt, and a liberal grinding of pepper. Process briefly to combine, and then scrape out into a bowl. Serve with your favorite pasta dish or soup. (This sauce can be stored for up to a week in the refrigerator.)

Yield: 2 cups of pesto (serves 8, ¼ cup each)

—*Cynthia Niles*

Tip: Since this recipe is high in calories, be sure to have it as a complement to a low-calorie pasta dish.

Per serving: 397 Cal.; 27 GI; 6g Prot.; 3g Carb.; 6g SFA; 24g MUFA; 9g PUFA; 0.3g Omega-3; 172mg Calc.; 196mg Sod.; 154mg Pot.; 2mg Iron; 0mg Phytoestrogen; 1g Fiber

2 cups chopped basil

4 cloves of garlic, chopped

1 cup pine nuts

1 cup olive oil

¾ cup freshly grated, reduced-fat Parmesan cheese

¼ cup freshly grated Romano cheese

Salt and pepper

Don't pass the cream!
Use non-fat sour cream or skim milk thickened with cornstarch instead of cream in pasta sauces. First dissolve cornstarch in a little cold water, then use 1 tablespoon of cornstarch for each 1 cup of liquid you are replacing. You can also use 1 tablespoon of flour whisked into 1 cup of non-fat milk as an alternative substitute for heavy cream.

pasta with braised garden vegetable ratatouille

 Here is a wonderful low-calorie pasta. Add a salad for a complete meal. You can replace the fresh tomato sauce with 28 ounces of your favorite low-sodium tomato sauce.

TOMATO SAUCE:

3 pounds plum tomatoes, cored

1 tablespoon olive oil

¼ large onion, diced

2 cloves of garlic, minced

½ cup finely chopped fresh basil

Salt and pepper

BRAISED VEGETABLES:

1 tablespoon olive oil

1 medium onion, diced

2 cloves of garlic, minced

1 medium summer squash, thinly sliced

1 medium zucchini, thinly sliced

1 medium eggplant, peeled and cubed

3 tablespoons finely chopped fresh basil

PASTA:

6 ounces pasta (long, flat pasta is best, such as fettuccine)

Salt and pepper

½ cup grated Parmesan cheese

To make the sauce, purée the tomatoes in a food processor and set aside.

Heat the olive oil in a 4-quart saucepan over medium heat. Add the onion and sauté for 5 minutes, or until tender and translucent. Add the garlic and sauté for 30 seconds, and then stir in the tomato purée and basil and simmer for 20 minutes over medium heat. Stir in the salt and pepper to taste.

While the tomato sauce is simmering, prepare the braised vegetables.

In a large, heavy saucepan, heat the olive oil over medium heat. Add the onion and sauté until tender and translucent. Add the garlic and sauté for an additional 30 seconds. Add the summer squash, zucchini, and eggplant and stir to combine, adding more oil if needed. Sprinkle with the basil and then stir in the tomato sauce and simmer for 30 minutes over low heat, stirring occasionally.

To make the pasta, cook it according to the package instructions. Drain the pasta and add it to the saucepan with the ratatouille. Toss well and add salt and pepper to taste if necessary. Garnish with the Parmesan cheese and serve immediately.

Yield: 4 servings

—*Brad Stevens, Tony Murillo, and Heather Tsatsarones, MS, RD, LDN*

Per serving: 409 Cal.; 47 GI; 17g Prot.; 60g Carb.; 4g SFA; 7g MUFA; 2g PUFA; 0.2g Omega-3; 277mg Calc.; 437mg Sod.; 1,628mg Pot.; 4mg Iron; 0mg Phytoestrogen; 13g Fiber

Entrées

pan-roasted haddock

 This is a great recipe with a truly Mediterranean flavor that you can pull together in no time.

1 (½-pound) haddock fillet

2 teaspoons olive oil, divided

1/8 teaspoon freshly ground pepper

½ tablespoon minced shallot

½ cup halved cherry tomatoes

1/8 cup chopped olives

½ tablespoon capers, rinsed and chopped

1 teaspoon dried oregano

½ teaspoon balsamic vinegar

Preheat the oven to 450°F.

Rub the haddock fillet with 1 teaspoon of the olive oil, sprinkle with the pepper, and place in a small roasting pan. Bake for about 15 minutes (the fish should easily flake with a fork).

While the fish is roasting, heat the remaining teaspoon of olive oil in a skillet over medium-high heat. Add the shallots and sauté for about 20 seconds. Add the tomatoes, olives, and capers and sauté for about 30 seconds, and then stir in the oregano and vinegar. Set aside and keep warm.

When the haddock is cooked, place it on a plate, spoon the warm tapenade over it, and serve.

Yield: 1 serving

—*Chef Jeffrey S. Merry*

Per serving: 263 Cal.; 51 GI; 44g Prot.; 9g Carb.; 1g SFA; 2g MUFA; 1g PUFA; 1g Omega-3; 93mg Calc.; 463mg Sod.; 987mg Pot.; 2mg Iron; 0.007mg Phytoestrogen; 3g Fiber

sautéed trout with citrus

 This flaky, juicy trout dish with a spritz of citrus is vibrant and refreshing.

To make the seasoning, combine the salt, chili powder, cumin, and coriander and store in a spice bottle.

Preheat the oven to 400°F. Spray a baking dish with cooking spray.

Season each fish fillet with ¼ teaspoon of the seasoning. Grill or bake the fish for 10 to 12 minutes, or until cooked through.

While the fish is cooking, divide the citrus sections equally into 4 small bowls and combine each with 2 tablespoons of the marmalade.

To serve, place a fillet of fish on individual serving plates and top each with the citrus sections mixture, green onions, and a sprig of cilantro.

Yield: 4 servings

—Chef Tres Hundertmark

Per serving: 286 Cal.; 39 GI; 37g Prot.; 11g Carb.; 3g SFA; 3g MUFA; 3g PUFA; 2g Omega-3; 64mg Calc.; 2,853mg Sod.; 1,041mg Pot.; 2mg Iron; 0.115mg Phytoestrogen; 2g Fiber

SEASONING:

1½ tablespoons salt

1 teaspoon chili powder

½ teaspoon ground cumin

½ teaspoon ground coriander

FISH:

Cooking spray

4 (6-ounce) fillets sunburst trout

1 ruby red grapefruit section, quartered

2 navel orange sections, halved

2 blood orange sections, halved

4 satsuma sections

½ cup orange marmalade, divided

2 green onions, sliced diagonally

4 sprigs of cilantro

olive oil–poached halibut with black chickpea tapenade

 This fish dish has a tasty and elegant pairing of ingredients and makes a beautiful presentation.

CHICKPEA TAPENADE:

2½ cups black chickpeas (soaked overnight)

4 quarts chicken broth (or vegetable broth)

1 onion, halved

1 carrot

1 clove of garlic

1 piece of pork (prosciuttto, bacon, ham hock) (optional)

3 tablespoons olive oil

2 ripe tomatoes, diced

1 red bell pepper, roasted, seeded, peeled, and diced

12 black olives, chopped

Zest of 2 lemons

6 tablespoons white balsamic vinegar

4 shallots, chopped

1 bunch of parsley, chopped

Salt and pepper

FISH:

4 quarts olive oil

6 (6-ounce) pieces of thick halibut

To make the chickpea tapenade, put the chickpeas in a large heavy saucepan. Add the broth, onion, carrot, garlic, and pork (if using). Bring to a boil and then reduce the heat and simmer, covered, for 1 to 2 hours, until the beans are tender. Drain and put the chickpeas in a large bowl. (Discard the onion, carrot, garlic, and pork.)

Heat the olive oil in a large saucepan over medium-high heat. Add the tomatoes, roasted bell pepper, olives, lemon zest, vinegar, shallots, and parsley and sauté until the vegetables are tender. Add this mixture to the bowl of chickpeas, season with salt and pepper to taste, and set aside in a warm place.

To make the fish, fill a saucepan (large enough to hold the fish in one layer) with the olive oil (enough to cover the fish), and heat to 130°F. Add the fish and poach for about 10 minutes, until the fish is cooked through. Place the fish in a serving dish and cover with the chickpea tapenade. Serve immediately.

Yield: 6 servings

—*Chef Neal Fraser*

Per serving: 764 Cal.; 45 GI; 48g Prot.; 65g Carb.; 5g SFA; 23g MUFA; 6g PUFA; 1g Omega-3; 156mg Calc.; 2,745mg Sod.; 1,289mg Pot.; 6mg Iron; 2mg Phytoestrogen; 15g Fiber

sweet-and-sour tuna

 Tuna is the number one fish in Sicily. This recipe, called *tonno agrodolce*, is common to the island's cuisine. It is sweet and sour in taste and is served rare, and it's sure to become your favorite new way of making tuna.

Rinse the tuna steaks, pat dry, and then coat them with the flour and salt to taste.

Heat the olive oil in a large skillet over medium heat. Add the onion and sauté until tender but not browned. Add the tuna steaks and cook for 4 minutes on each side. Add the vinegar, marsala, raisins, olives, and bay leaves and cook for an additional 7 minutes. Turn off the heat, cover the skillet, and let rest for 10 minutes for the flavor of the sauce to be absorbed by the tuna. Before serving, discard the bay leaves.

Yield: 4 servings

—*Karen's Cucina*

Per serving: 282 Cal.; 63 GI; 18g Prot.; 20g Carb.; 2g SFA; 9g MUFA; 2g PUFA; 0.5g Omega-3; 47mg Calc.; 556mg Sod.; 459mg Pot.; 1mg Iron; 0.34mg Phytoestrogen; 2g Fiber

4 tuna steaks

All-purpose flour for coating

Salt

3 tablespoons extra-virgin olive oil

1 large onion, sliced

½ cup red wine vinegar

3 tablespoons marsala

½ cup golden raisins

12 large pitted green olives

3 bay leaves

swordfish with orange-lemon sauce

 This recipe not only looks fantastic, it also tastes fantastic.

4 swordfish steaks

½ cup freshly squeezed lemon juice

½ cup freshly squeezed orange juice

1 cup finely chopped onion

3 cloves of garlic cloves, finely chopped

Handful of chopped Italian parsley

Zest of 1 lemon

Zest of 1 orange

Salt and pepper

Preheat oven to 375°F.

Place the swordfish steaks in a glass baking dish. Add the lemon and orange juices, onion, garlic, parsley, lemon and orange zests, and salt and pepper to taste. Turn the swordfish steaks to ensure they are well coated and bake for 20 minutes. Serve with the sauce spooned over top of the fish.

Yield: 4 servings

—*Karen's Cucina*

Per serving: 268 Cal.; 51 GI; 34g Prot.; 11g Carb.; 2g SFA; 3g MUFA; 3g PUFA; 2g Omega-3; 46mg Calc.; 98mg Sod.; 965mg Pot.; 1mg Iron; 0.08mg Phytoestrogen; 1g Fiber

halibut in wine and tomatoes

 This halibut has a succulent sauce and is surprisingly simple and elegant.

Heat the olive oil in a large saucepan over medium-high heat. Add the onion, garlic, and red pepper flakes and sauté until the onion is tender. Reduce the heat to medium and add the halibut, tomatoes, and wine. Cover and cook for 8 minutes. Stir in the parsley and salt and pepper to taste and serve.

Yield: 4 servings

—*Karen's Cucina*

Per serving: 378 Cal.; 55 GI; 34g Prot.; 14g Carb.; 2g SFA; 10g MUFA; 2g PUFA; 1g Omega-3; 111mg Calc.; 431mg Sod.; 971mg Pot.; 3mg Iron; 0.032mg Phytoestrogen; 3g Fiber

¼ cup olive oil

1 cup chopped onion

3 cloves of garlic, thinly sliced

Pinch of red pepper flakes

4 (6-ounce) halibut fillets

1 (28-ounce) can tomatoes

1 cup dry white wine

1/3 cup chopped Italian parsley

Salt and pepper

Avoid skipping meals

Skipping meals can affect your memory and concentration. Remember when your mom said, "You can't start your day on an empty stomach"? She was right. Antioxidant-rich foods such as blueberries and vegetables help slow down those memory lapses.

cod with rosemary and anchovies

 This recipe is very quick and easy to make and it has fantastic flavors and is delicious and nutritious as well.

3 tablespoons olive oil, divided

1 (2-ounce) can anchovy fillets

1 (3 to 4-pound) whole codfish

4 sprigs of rosemary, plus extra chopped

4 basil leaves, torn, plus extra chopped

½ cup bread crumbs

Salt and pepper

1 cup pitted black olives

Preheat the oven to 400°F. With olive oil, lightly grease a baking dish large enough to hold the fish.

Heat 2 tablespoons of the olive oil in a small skillet over medium-low heat. Add the anchovies, mashing them with a wooden spoon, and cook them until they almost disintegrate. Set aside.

Place the codfish in the greased baking dish and spoon half the anchovies inside the cavity. Add the rosemary sprigs and torn basil leaves, and drizzle the remaining 1 tablespoon of olive oil over the fish. Spoon the remaining anchovies over the fish and sprinkle with the chopped rosemary and basil and the bread crumbs. Season with salt and pepper to taste and bake, uncovered, for 30 minutes. Serve with olives.

Yield: 4 servings

—*Karen's Cucina*

Per serving: 467 Cal.; 70 GI; 59g Prot.; 12g Carb.; 3g SFA; 11g MUFA; 3g PUFA; 2g Omega-3; 128mg Calc.; 1,039mg Sod.; 867mg Pot.; 3mg Iron; 0.1mg Phytoestrogen; 2g Fiber

red snapper with tomatoes

This is an incredibly simple recipe with a Mediterranean flair, and it's fragrant and delicious with a great gourmet taste.

Heat the olive oil in a large skillet over low heat. Add the garlic and cook for about 3 minutes, until the garlic is tender. Add the tomatoes, mashing them with a wooden spoon, and salt and pepper to taste and cook an additional 10 minutes. Add the red snapper and simmer for 20 minutes longer on one side only (do not turn the fish over). Sprinkle with the parsley and serve.

Yield: 6 servings

—*Karen's Cucina*

Per serving: 375 Cal.; 50 GI; 55g Prot.; 6g Carb.; 2g SFA; 8g MUFA; 2g PUFA; 1g Omega-3; 98mg Calc.; 403mg Sod.; 1,063mg Pot.; 3mg Iron; 0mg Phytoestrogen; 2g Fiber

3 tablespoons extra-virgin olive oil

2 cloves of garlic, thinly sliced

1 (16-ounce) can Italian tomatoes

Salt and pepper

2½ pounds red snapper fillets

Handful of chopped Italian parsley

salmon with pomegranate caponata and fennel slaw

 Salmon is one of the richest sources of omega-3s, the king of fish oils. Eating salmon helps to keep our arteries clear and our heart strong. This recipe is not only tasty and unique, but it's healthy as well.

CAPONATA:

2 tablespoons olive oil

2 cloves of garlic, minced

2 tablespoons minced shallots

2 tablespoons peeled and minced ginger

½ cup pomegranate seeds

2 tablespoons non-pareil capers, strained

1 tablespoon lemon juice

2 tablespoons finely chopped cilantro

2 tablespoons finely chopped Italian parsley

Salt and pepper

FENNEL SLAW:

1 head of fennel, cored and sliced paper-thin

2 tablespoons olive oil

Juice of 1 lemon

2 tablespoons snipped dill

Salt and pepper

To make the caponata, heat the oil in a small skillet over medium heat. Add the garlic, shallots, and ginger and sauté for 4 minutes, until tender. Stir in the pomegranate seeds and remove from the heat. Mix in the capers, lemon juice, cilantro, and parsley and season with salt and pepper to taste. Set aside.

To make the fennel slaw, combine the fennel, olive oil, lemon juice, cilantro, parsley, and salt and pepper to taste in a large bowl. Mix well and set aside.

To make the salmon, preheat the oven to 375°F. Lightly grease a baking dish.

Heat the grape seed oil in a skillet over medium-high heat. Season the salmon fillets with salt and pepper and place them in the skillet, skin side down, and cook until golden. Then place the fillets in the greased baking dish, keeping the skin side down, and bake for 5 minutes for medium rare to medium.

To serve, spoon the fennel slaw onto 4 individual serving plates, place a fillet of fish on top of the salad, and top with the caponata.

Yield: 4 servings

—*Michelle Bernstein*

Per serving: 409 Cal.; 51 GI; 38g Prot.; 6g Carb.; 3g SFA; 10g MUFA; 8g PUFA; 2g Omega-3; 24mg Calc.; 234mg Sod.; 718mg Pot.; 1mg Iron; 0mg Phytoestrogen; 1g Fiber

SALMON:

2 tablespoons grape seed oil

4 (6-ounce) fillets of wild salmon (preferably with the skin)

Salt and pepper

wild alaskan halibut crusted with brioche with a salad of french green beans, belgian endive, watercress, and tomatoes

 This is a delicious early spring and summer dish to enjoy! A few notes: If you can't find wild Alaskan halibut, you can use any white-fleshed fish. You can use brioche buns, rolls, or a loaf. Extra-virgin olive oil can be substituted for the hazelnut oil. Sherry wine vinegar has a mild and distinctive flavor; however, you may use red wine vinegar instead. Pole beans may be substituted for the French beans.

SALAD:

½ pound French green beans, trimmed

2 Roma tomatoes

2 white Belgian endives

1 bunch of watercress (tender-leaf or hydroponic)

Salt and freshly ground pepper

2 tablespoons hazelnut oil

2 teaspoons sherry wine vinegar

HALIBUT:

½ pound brioche bread

½ stick unsalted butter (2 ounces)

2 (7-ounce) fillets wild Alaskan halibut

Salt and cracked pepper

To make the salad, in a pot of boiling salted water, blanch the beans, remove from the water with a slotted spoon, and refresh them in ice-cold water. Set aside and keep the water boiling.

Core the tomatoes and score a small X on the top of each tomato. Place them in the boiling water and blanch them for a moment, lift them out with a slotted spoon and refresh under cold running water, and then, with a sharp knife, peel away and discard the skin. Cut off the top of the tomatoes in a petal shape and scoop out and discard the seeds. Cut the tomatoes into julienne strips and set aside.

Split the endives in half, core them, and then cut them into julienne strips. Place a wet paper towel on top and set aside.

Place the endives, tomatoes, beans, and watercress in a salad bowl. Season to taste with the salt and freshly ground pepper and set the salad aside. Whisk together the oil and vinegar and set aside.

To make the fish, cut up the brioche and toast until lightly golden brown, and then place in a food processor and process to make bread crumbs and set aside on a plate.

Clarify the butter by melting it in a small saucepan over low heat. Skim off the foam that rises to the top, and once the solids settle in the bottom, remove the clear butter and discard the milk solids. Keep the clarified butter warm.

Season the halibut fillets with salt and cracked pepper to taste and set aside. Put half the clarified butter in a Teflon or stainless steel skillet and heat over medium-high heat. Dip the fish fillets into the remaining clarified butter, and then into the brioche crumbs. Reduce the heat to medium and place the fillets in the skillet and cook for about 3 minutes on each side, until golden brown on both sides. (If the fillets are very thick, place them in a 375°F oven and bake for 5 minutes to cook through.) Remove the fish from the skillet and let them rest on a paper towel to remove the excess fat.

To serve, toss the oil and vinegar dressing with the salad, place the fish on individual serving plates, top each with the salad, and serve!

Yield: 2 servings

—*Carrie Nahabedian*

Per serving: 867 Cal.; 71 GI; 56g Prot.; 95g Carb.; 7g SFA; 14g MUFA; 5g PUFA; 1g Omega-3; 301mg Calc.; 1,010mg Sod.; 1,339mg Pot.; 8mg Iron; 1mg Phytoestrogen; 11g Fiber

wild snapper mediterranean with artichokes à la barigoule, valencia oranges, french green beans, and basil

 The fresh vegetables and mild seasonings in this recipe complement the depth of flavor of the snapper without overpowering the sweetness. The presentation of the dish is just as impressive as the taste!

2 artichokes

2 tablespoons salt

½ lemon

7 tablespoons olive oil, divided

1 leek, white with a touch of green, split, cleaned and cut into ¼-inch slices

½ medium yellow onion, halved and thinly sliced

1 rib of celery, thinly sliced

1 carrot, peeled, channel cut, and thinly sliced

Salt and cracked peppercorns

1¼ cups water

¼ cup white wine

1 bay leaf

A few sprigs of thyme

5 peppercorns

A few stems of parsley

4 cloves of garlic

½ teaspoon salt

4 (4 to 5-ounce) fillets of red snapper, skin on

½ pound French green beans, blanched

All the vegetables are for garnish and should be cut with care and attention.

Trim and clean the artichokes, leaving the bottom and heart intact. Place the artichokes in a deep stainless steel saucepan with fresh cold water to cover and the salt and half lemon. Cover with a white napkin or cloth and cook over medium-high heat until tender. Remove the artichokes from the water and cool immediately under cold running water. Cut the artichokes in half, remove and discard the chokes, and then cut the artichokes into quarters. Set aside.

Heat 3 tablespoons of the olive oil in a large, heavy saucepan over low heat. Add the leek, onion, celery, and carrot and cover the saucepan and sweat the vegetables until they are just tender. Season with salt and cracked peppercorns to taste, and then add the water and white wine to cover the vegetables. Make a bouquet garni by tieing the bay leaf, thyme sprigs, peppercorns, and parsley stems in a cheesecloth bag and place it in the saucepan. Bring to a boil, and then reduce the heat and simmer the "barigoule" over medium heat until the carrots are tender. Remove from the heat and place the pan in an ice bath to cool.

Place the garlic cloves in a small saucepan, cover with water, and bring to a quick boil. Refresh under cold water and repeat the process 3 times. In the final cooking, add ½ teaspoon of salt. Cool the now "sweet" garlic cloves under cold water, slice thinly, and set aside.

Heat 1 tablespoon of the olive oil in a non-stick or heavy skillet over medium-high heat. Season the fish fillets with salt and pepper and place, flesh side down, in the skillet. Sear the fish for about 2 minutes, or until golden brown, and then turn and cook on the skin side for an additional 3 minutes. With a spoon, baste the fish with the olive oil and cooking juices for added flavor and color. Set aside and keep warm.

To finish the beautiful dish, pour the "barigoule" broth and vegetables into a casserole. Bring to a boil, lower the heat, and stir in the remaining 3 tablespoons of olive oil. Garnish with the artichokes, French green beans, tomatoes, sweet garlic, Valencia oranges, and basil. Place the fish in a deep bowl, spoon the "barigoule" over top, and serve immediately.

Yield: 4 servings

—*Carrie Nahabedian*

Per serving: 342 Cal.; 48 GI; 11g Prot.; 29g Carb.; 3g SFA; 15g MUFA; 2g PUFA; 0.4g Omega-3; 107mg Calc.; 89mg Sod.; 782mg Pot.; 2mg Iron; 0mg Phytoestrogen; 10g Fiber

2 tomatoes, peeled, seeded, and thinly sliced

2 Valencia oranges, peeled and segmented

3 sprigs of basil, cut into long, thin strips

soy grilled salmon skewers

 This delicious salmon recipe is easy to prepare and impressive looking for dinner guests. You can buy furikake seasoning at most oriental grocers; it is available vegetarian style or with dehydrated egg or shrimp.

1 (1-pound) salmon fillet, sliced lengthwise into 4 (1-inch) strips

½ cup soy sauce

½ cup freshly squeezed orange juice

¼ cup freshly squeezed lime juice

1 tablespoon minced ginger

1 clove of garlic, minced

1 teaspoon red pepper flakes

1 teaspoon furikake (seaweed and sesame rice seasoning)

Soak 4 bamboo skewers in water for 30 minutes, and then thread each salmon strip onto a soaked skewer and place in a shallow dish.

In a bowl, whisk together the soy sauce, orange juice, lime juice, ginger, garlic, red pepper flakes, and furikake. Pour ½ cup of the soy mixture over the skewers, turning to coat. Let marinate for 30 minutes. Save the remaining marinade for dipping.

Preheat an outdoor grill to medium-high heat.

Oil your grill generously, and then cook the skewers for 2 minutes per side, brushing often with the marinade, or until the fish starts to flake. Let them rest for 2 minutes before serving. Serve with the remaining marinade for dipping.

Yield: 4 servings

—*Donnie Ferneau Jr.*

Per serving: 266 Cal.; 45 GI; 33g Prot.; 10g Carb.; 1g SFA; 3g MUFA; 4g PUFA; 3g Omega-3; 36mg Calc.; 2,468mg Sod.; 962mg Pot.; 2mg Iron; 0.6mg Phytoestrogen; 1g Fiber

broiled george's bank codfish with citrus and fennel slaw

 This is a favorite dish at the Black Dog Café on Martha's Vineyard that you can make at home. It's delicious and light and doesn't take long to prepare. For convenience, you can make the slaw the day before and refrigerate until the fish is cooked.

To make the slaw, place the fennel shavings and fronds, orange and grapefruit segments, and the fennel seeds in a salad bowl. In a small bowl, whisk together the olive oil, vinegar, and mustard and toss with the fennel mixture. Set aside.

To make the fish, preheat the oven to 350°F. Place the codfish in a shallow baking dish and season with salt and pepper to taste. Pour the wine and lemon juice over top and bake for 8 to 10 minutes, until opaque. Serve immediately with the citrus and fennel slaw.

Yield: 4 servings

—Chef Bill Hart

Per serving (fish): 148 Cal.; 36 GI; 2g Prot.; 21g Carb.; 1g SFA; 5g MUFA; 1g PUFA; 0g Omega-3; 83mg Calc.; 46mg Sod.; 390mg Pot.; 0.6mg Iron; 0mg Phytoestrogen; 5g Fiber

Per serving (slaw): 221 Cal.; 45 GI; 42g Prot.; 1g Carb.; 0.6g SFA; 0.4g MUFA; 1g PUFA; 1g Omega-3; 34mg Calc.; 187mg Sod.; 628mg Pot.; 0.6mg Iron; 0mg Phytoestrogen; 0g Fiber

SLAW:

1 cup shaved fennel (paper thin)

1 tablespoon chopped fennel fronds (tops)

3 navel oranges, segmented

1 pink grapefruit, segmented

1 tablespoon toasted fennel seeds

2 tablespoons olive oil

2 tablespoons sherry vinegar

1 teaspoon whole-grain mustard

FISH:

4 (8-ounce) cod fillets

Salt and pepper

2 tablespoons lemon juice

¼ cup dry white wine

hamachi en escabeche

 This recipe has gotten rave reviews from many restaurant critics.

AJO BLANCO PURÉE:

¼ cup extra-virgin olive oil

6 cloves of garlic, thinly sliced

2 basil leaves

¼ cup sliced baguette, crusts removed

½ cup roasted Marcona almonds

2 cups spring water

1 tablespoon kosher salt

1 tablespoon aged sherry vinegar

BLACK OLIVE ESCABECHE:

¼ cup pitted Kalamata olives

¼ cup honey

¼ cup white wine vinegar

3 sprigs of thyme, leaves chopped

2 shallots, very finely chopped

To make the ajo blanco purée, heat the olive oil in a small saucepan over medium-low heat. Add the garlic and basil and sauté until the garlic turns light golden. Remove from the heat and discard the basil. Add the sliced baguette to the oil and let soak for a few minutes. When the oil mixture is cool, place it in a food processor with the almonds and spring water and purée for at least 5 minutes. Strain through a fine mesh strainer and chill for at least 4 hours, or until the purée is thick and mousse-like.

To make the black olive escabeche, combine all the ingredients, mix well, and refrigerate.

To assemble the dish, toss the cucumber blossoms with ½ cup of the black olive escabeche and let it marinate for at least 5 minutes. Heat the blended oil in a skillet over high heat. Season the hamachi loin generously with salt and pepper and place in the skillet. Sear the hamachi on one side until lightly caramelized, but still raw. Remove from the heat and slice the fish into 4 equal pieces. Place 2 tablespoons of the ajo blanco purée on each of 4 individual serving plates. Place a slice of fish on top of the purée. Spoon 3 cucumber blossoms and one-quarter of the black olive escabeche mixture on and around each serving of fish. Serve immediately.

Yield: 4 servings

—Chef de Cuisine Michael Fiorello

Per serving: 581 Cal.; 61 GI; 25g Prot.; 30g Carb.; 5g SFA; 26g MUFA; 6g PUFA; 1g Omega-3; 127mg Calc.; 1,009mg Sod.; 523mg Pot.; 4mg Iron; 0mg Phytoestrogen; 4g Fiber

¼ cup extra-virgin olive oil

1½ teaspoons kosher salt

¼ teaspoon freshly ground pepper

¼ bunch of parsley, chopped

5 roasted cloves of garlic, mashed

HAMACHI:

12 cucumber blossoms

½ cup black olive escabeche (above)

¼ cup blended oil

1 (12-ounce) hamachi loin (yellowtail tuna)

Kosher salt and freshly ground pepper

½ cup ajo blanco purée (above)

sautéed day-boat scallops, nettles, sunchokes, and raisin-caper emulsion

 Impress your guests with this sophisticated entrée that includes the finest of ingredients.

NETTLES:

4 ounces nettles, stems removed (wear gloves)

2 tablespoons olive oil

¼ cup water

Kosher salt

SUNCHOKES:

2 tablespoons olive oil

2 sunchokes, peeled and sliced with a mandolin slicer

Kosher salt

RAISIN-CAPER SAUCE:

2/3 cup sultana (golden) raisins

2 tablespoons capers

2 tablespoons sherry wine vinegar

½ cup water

SCALLOPS:

4 large (size U-10) dry-packed day-boat scallops

Kosher salt

Canola oil

2 tablespoons butter

To prepare the nettles (make sure you wear gloves when handling nettles as they will sting your hands), in a saucepan, combine the nettles, olive oil, water, and salt to taste and cook over medium-low heat for about 10 minutes, until the nettles are tender. Set aside.

To prepare the sunchokes, heat the olive oil in a skillet over medium-high heat. Add the sunchokes and sauté until golden brown. Season with salt to taste and set aside.

To make the sauce, put the raisins, capers, vinegar, and water in a saucepan and simmer until the raisins are rehydrated. If the mixture becomes too dry, add some more water. Blend in a food processor and set aside.

To make the scallops, season them with salt to taste. Heat a skillet over high heat until hot, and then add the canola oil and then immediately add the scallops. Sauté for 30 seconds. Add the butter and continue to cook until the bottom side of the scallops are golden brown. Flip the scallops, reduce the heat, and cook for another 2 minutes. Remove from the skillet and pat dry.

To serve, spoon the sauce onto each of 4 individual serving plates, then the nettles, then the scallops, and top each with the sunchokes. Serve immediately.

Yield: 4 servings

—Chef Neal Fraser

Per serving: 318 Cal.; 61 GI; 6g Prot.; 29g Carb.; 2g SFA; 15g MUFA; 3g PUFA; 0.8g Omega-3; 97mg Calc.; 853mg Sod.; 512mg Pot.; 2mg Iron; 0.052mg Phytoestrogen; 3g Fiber

orange scallops

If you are looking for an easy scallop dish to make, this is a winner. The combination of tomatoes and orange create a magical flavor and glamour.

Heat 3 tablespoons of the olive oil in a medium-sized saucepan over medium heat. Add the garlic and leek and sauté for about 10 minutes, until the leek is tender. Add the tomatoes with their juice, the salt, orange zest, and cayenne and bring to a boil. Reduce the heat and simmer for about 7 minutes, until the sauce begins to thicken.

Rinse the scallops and pat dry, and then coat them lightly with the flour. If the scallops are large, cut them in half.

In a large skillet, heat the remaining 1 tablespoon of olive oil over medium-high heat. Add the scallops and sauté until lightly golden. Stir in the tomato sauce mixture and cook for about 3 minutes, until heated through. Add salt if needed.

Yield: 4 servings

—*Karen's Cucina*

Per serving: 248 Cal.; 63 GI; 16g Prot.; 21g Carb.; 2g SFA; 7g MUFA; 1.5g PUFA; 0.3 g Omega-3; 135mg Calc.; 730mg Sod.; 674mg Pot.; 4mg Iron; 0mg Phytoestrogen; 3g Fiber

4 tablespoons extra-virgin olive oil, divided

1 leek, trimmed, rinsed, and thinly sliced

3 cloves of garlic, finely chopped

1 (28-ounce) can tomatoes, chopped

Pinch of salt

Pinch of cayenne

1 teaspoon orange zest

1 pound sea scallops

½ cup all-purpose flour

shrimp in tomato sauce with capers

 This is a delicious and aromatic Sicilian dish with a combination of excellent ingredients. Your guests will want this recipe for sure.

1½ pounds shrimp

½ cup extra-virgin olive oil

1 medium red onion, finely chopped

3 cloves of garlic, finely chopped

1 large rib of celery, finely chopped

1 small carrot, pared and finely chopped

1 (28-ounce) can Italian tomatoes

Salt and pepper

5 tablespoons raisins

5 tablespoons pine nuts

6 tablespoons capers, drained

6 bay leaves

Handful of chopped basil

Handful of chopped Italian parsley

1 lemon, cut into 4 wedges

Preheat the oven to 375°F.

Wash and drain the shrimp. Set aside in ice-cold water.

Heat the olive oil in a medium-sized skillet over medium heat. Add the onion, garlic, celery, and carrot and sauté for 10 minutes, until the vegetables are tender. Add the tomatoes, smashing them with a wooden spoon, and cook for 15 minutes longer. Season with salt and pepper to taste.

Meanwhile, soak the raisins in small bowl of warm water for 10 minutes. Then drain them and add them and the pine nuts and capers to the skillet and cook for an additional 10 minutes.

Transfer the tomato mixture to a glass baking dish. Drain the shrimp and place them over the tomato sauce, and then place the bay leaves over the shrimp. Cover the baking dish with aluminum foil and bake for 10 minutes. Remove the dish from the oven, discard the bay leaves, and gently mix the shrimp into the tomato sauce. Serve sprinkled with the basil and parsley and with the lemon wedges on the side.

Yield: 4 servings

—Karen's Cucina

Per serving: 533 Cal.; 55 GI; 31g Prot.; 26g Carb.; 5g SFA; 22g MUFA; 7g PUFA; 1g Omega-3; 168mg Calc.; 1,205mg Sod.; 960mg Pot.; 8mg Iron; 0.028mg Phytoestrogen; 5g Fiber

seafood couscous paella

Whole-wheat couscous soaks up the savory saffron-infused broth. Besides scallops and shrimp, halibut, Dover sole, and red snapper also work well in this dish.

Heat the olive oil in a large saucepan over medium heat. Add the onions and garlic and sauté for 3 to 4 minutes, until tender but not browned. Add the thyme, fennel, salt, white pepper, and saffron and cook for a few minutes longer. Stir in the tomatoes and broth and bring to a boil. Reduce the heat and simmer, covered, for 5 minutes. Increase the heat again to medium and stir in the scallops and shrimp. Cook for 6 to 8 minutes, stirring occasionally. Stir in the couscous, cover, and remove from heat. Let stand for 5 minutes, until the couscous is tender. Fluff with a large fork and serve immediately.

Yield: 4 servings

—Chef Aldo

Per serving: 399 Cal.; 61 GI; 22g Prot.; 43g Carb.; 2g SFA; 10g MUFA; 2g PUFA; 0.3g Omega-3; 88mg Calc.; 806mg Sod.; 589mg Pot.; 3mg Iron; 0mg Phytoestrogen; 4g Fiber

4 tablespoons extra-virgin olive oil

2 medium onions, chopped

2 cloves of garlic, minced

2 teaspoons dried thyme

1 teaspoon ground fennel

1 teaspoon kosher salt

Pinch of white pepper

2 pinches of saffron

2 cups diced canned tomatoes and their juice

½ cup vegetable broth

½ pound bay scallops

½ pound small bay shrimp, peeled and deveined

1 cup whole-wheat couscous

seared hand-harvested maine sea scallops with caramelized onions, savoy cabbage, french lentils, and balsamic syrup

 You can obtain fresh diver sea scallops from a high-quality fish source. If these are unavailable, use the fresh sea scallops at your local grocery store. Scallops are available in a few sizes, try to get the "10" or "10 and up" count.

2 pounds French du Puy lentils (or green lentils)

Chicken broth or water

1 small carrot

1 rib of celery

¼ onion

1 head of savoy cabbage

½ cup olive oil

2 yellow onions, thinly sliced

Salt

2 cups balsamic vinegar

2 scallops per person as an appetizer or 4 as an entrée

Cracked peppercorns

½ bunch of parsley, chopped

Put the lentils in a large saucepan and add the chicken broth or water to cover. Stir in the carrot, celery, and onion and bring to a boil. Reduce the heat and simmer, covered, for about 45 minutes, or until the lentils are tender.

Remove and discard the outer leaves of the cabbage, leaving the inner yellows leaves. Remove and discard the core and blanch the leaves in boiling salted water, and then refresh them in ice water. Cut the leaves into long, thin strips and set aside.

Heat the olive oil in a small skillet over high heat. Add the onions and sauté with care, stirring constantly, until the onions are glazed and caramelized. Season with salt to taste and set aside.

In a heavy saucepan, reduce the balsamic vinegar over medium-high heat until the consistency is of syrup. Take care not to burn the vinegar. Keep at room temperature or warmer if you are going to use it immediately. It can be refrigerated indefinitely and warmed up as needed.

Pat the scallops dry and season with salt and cracked pepper. Sear in a heavy skillet over medium-high to high heat, browning the scallops on all sides. (If necessary, they can be placed in a medium oven for a few minutes to complete cooking.)

Mix the onions and cabbage together and place on individual serving plates and top each with some of the lentils. Place the scallops on top, and if there are any pan juices from the scallops, spoon a touch or two over each serving. Drizzle each dish with the balsamic syrup and garnish with the chopped parsley. Serve immediately.

Yield: 8 scallops for 2 servings

—Carrie Nahabedian

Per serving: 1,190 Cal.; 27 GI; 72g Prot.; 156g Carb.; 4g SFA; 21g MUFA; 4g PUFA; 0.7g Omega-3; 255mg Calc.; 219mg Sod.; 2,937mg Pot.; 24mg Iron; 0.05mg Phytoestrogen; 39g Fiber

lobster and duck chow mein

 Fortified with an abundance of fresh ingredients, this is a delectable new way to enjoy chow mein.

BBQ DUCK MARINADE:

2 cinnamon sticks

¼ cup coriander seeds

¼ cup star anise

5 cloves

5 whole allspice

½ teaspoon red pepper flakes

¼ cup Szechwan peppercorns

4 cups hoisin sauce

4 cups soy sauce

1½ cups sesame oil

1 cup rice wine vinegar

Zest of 2 oranges

1 stalk of lemongrass

1 small bunch of green onions, chopped

1 tablespoon minced ginger

1 tablespoon minced garlic

½ pound duck, cut into 4 pieces

CHOW MEIN SAUCE:

1 cup Chinese BBQ sauce

1 cup oyster sauce

1½ cups hoisin sauce

½ cup black soy sauce

To make the BBQ duck marinade, preheat the oven to 350°F. Place the cinnamon, coriander, anise, cloves, allspice, red pepper flakes, and peppercorns on a baking sheet and toast in the oven for 2 minutes. Combine the hoisin sauce, soy sauce, sesame oil, and vinegar in a large bowl and mix well. Stir in the toasted spices, orange zest, lemongrass, green onions, ginger, and garlic. Add the duck pieces and marinate in the refrigerator for 12 to 24 hours.

To make the chow mein sauce, combine the BBQ sauce, hoisin sauce, soy sauce, sambal oelek, chili sauce, water, and sugar in a large bowl. Mix well and set aside.

To make the entrée, remove the duck from the marinade and pat dry. Heat the peanut oil in a wok over high heat. Add the marinated duck and the lobster and sauté for 1 minute, and then move them to the side of the wok. Add the celery, carrots, mushrooms, garlic, shallots, and ginger and sauté until

What happents to your body when you eat a large meal?
The body's digestion brings blood into the abdomen, raises body temperature, and voilà, tells the hypothalamus part of the brain to send a signal that causes hot flashes. Eating smaller meals can help reduce the number of hot flashes.

the vegetables are tender. Add the chow mein sauce and the cooked noodles and sauté for 1 minute longer, stirring constantly. Garnish with the bean sprouts, chives, bell pepper, cilantro, and pepper rings. Serve immediately.

Yield: 4 servings

—*Chef Brad Parsons*

Per serving (about 2 tablespoons) (BBQ Duck Marinade): 254 Cal.; 84 GI; 4.5g Prot.; 24g Carb.; 2g SFA; 6g MUFA; 6g PUFA; 1g Omega-3; 42mg Calc.; 3,087mg Sod.; 197mg Pot.; 2mg Iron; 5mg Phytoestrogen; 2g Fiber

Per serving (about 2 tablespoons) (Chow Mein Sauce): 68 Cal.; 79 GI; 1g Prot.; 14g Carb.; 0.1g SFA; 0.1g MUFA; 0.2g PUFA; 0g Omega-3; 17mg Calc.; 1,055mg Sod.; 112mg Pot.; 0.5mg Iron; 1.5mg Phytoestrogen; 1g Fiber

Per serving (Entrée): 600 Cal.; 41 GI; 37g Prot.; 89g Carb.; 2g SFA; 3g MUFA; 3g PUFA; 0.2g Omega-3; 104mg Calc.; 281mg Sod.; 676mg Pot.; 6mg Iron; 0mg Phytoestrogen; 6g Fiber

2 tablespoons sambal oelek

¼ cup Thai sweet chili sauce

¼ cup water

¼ cup sugar

ENTRÉE:

1 tablespoon peanut oil

½ pound lobster (claw and knuckle), chopped

¾ cup julienned celery

¾ cup julienned carrots

½ pound shiitake mushrooms, sliced

4 teaspoons minced shallots

4 teaspoons minced garlic

4 teaspoons minced ginger

24 ounces egg noodles, prepared per package instructions

GARNISHES:

Bean sprouts

Garlic chives, chopped

Red bell pepper, julienned

Cilantro, minced

Fresno pepper rings

chicken and shrimp sorentina

 Treat yourself to one of Liberatore's delicious and time-tested recipes.

4 boneless chicken breasts, pounded thin

All-purpose flour for dredging

1 tablespoon margarine

10 to 12 jumbo shrimp

16 to 20 artichoke hearts, quartered

1 ripe tomato, diced

1½ teaspoons rubbed sage

1 tablespoon dried parsley

1 cup dry white wine

1 cup chicken broth

Salt and pepper

8 slices prosciutto

8 slices mozzarella cheese

Dredge the chicken in the flour. Heat the margarine in a large skillet over medium heat. Add the chicken and shrimp and sauté until the chicken is brown on one side. Add the artichoke hearts and tomatoes. Turn the chicken breasts and brown on the other side. Add the sage, parsley, and wine and simmer for 4 to 5 minutes. Add the broth, reduce the heat to low, and simmer for a few minutes more. Season with salt and pepper to taste and top with the prosciutto and mozzarella and continue to simmer until the cheese melts. Serve with lots of love over linguine and enjoy!

Yield: 4 servings

—*John Liberatore*

Per serving: 509 Cal.; 49 GI; 57g Prot.; 26g Carb.; 6g SFA; 5g MUFA; 2g PUFA; 0.4g Omega-3; 289mg Calc.; 1,570mg Sod.; 1,186mg Pot.; 4mg Iron; 0mg Phytoestrogen; 16g Fiber

chicken giovanni

 This is a delicious dish that you will enjoy making and eating, and you'll plan on making it again.

Melt the margarine in a skillet over medium-high heat. Lightly dust the chicken breasts in the flour and place in the skillet. Add the rosemary sprigs. Lightly brown the chicken on both sides. Add the wines and lemon juice. Lower the heat and simmer for 8 to 9 minutes. Add the broth and let simmer for an additional 8 to 9 minutes to reduce the broth.

Meanwhile, steam or boil the spinach until tender, and when the chicken is almost done, season with salt and pepper to taste and place half the spinach on top of each chicken breast. Top each with a slice of mozzarella and melt. Serve immediately.

Yield: 2 servings

—John Liberatore

Per serving: 360 Cal.; 59 GI; 34g Prot.; 15g Carb.; 4g SFA; 4g MUFA; 3g PUFA; 0.4g Omega-3; 189mg Calc.; 333mg Sod.; 678mg Pot.; 3mg Iron; 0mg Phytoestrogen; 2g Fiber

1 tablespoon margarine

2 boneless, skinless chicken breasts

All-purpose flour for dusting chicken

2 sprigs of rosemary

¼ cup white wine

¼ cup sherry wine

Juice of ½ lemon

½ cup chicken broth

¾ cup chopped spinach

Salt and pepper

2 slices mozzarella cheese

curry chicken

 The aroma of this easy-to-prepare recipe will make your guests think you spent hours in the kitchen.

2 cups rice

1 tablespoon curry powder

1 tablespoon ground cinnamon

1 teaspoon ground ginger

¼ teaspoon red pepper flakes

2 tablespoons olive oil

1 onion, chopped

3 to 4 boneless chicken breasts, cut into bite-sized pieces

2 to 3 heads of broccoli

1 low-sodium chicken bouillon cube

1 (8-ounce) can reduced-fat coconut milk

1 tablespoon minced garlic

Salt and pepper

Cook the rice according to the package instructions and set aside.

In a small bowl, combine the curry, cinnamon, ginger, and red pepper flakes and set aside.

Heat the oil in a large saucepan over medium-high heat. Add the onion and chicken and cook until the chicken is done.

Meanwhile, steam the broccoli until tender. When the chicken is done, add the spices, coconut milk, and bouillon cube to the chicken. Bring to a gentle boil, add the broccoli, and cook to heat through. Serve over the cooked rice.

Yield: 4 servings

—*Cynthia Niles*

Per serving: 557 Cal.; 54 GI; 36g Prot.; 84g Carb.; 2g SFA; 3g MUFA; 3g PUFA; 0.2g Omega-3; 208mg Calc.; 151mg Sod.; 609mg Pot.; 4mg Iron; 11mg Phytoestrogen; 14g Fiber

moroccan chicken over apricot-cranberry couscous

 The exciting spices in this recipe will fill your kitchen with a wonderfully savory aroma. Apricot-cranberry couscous is a sweet, healthy side dish that perfectly complements the chicken dish.

To make the chicken, combine all ingredients except the chicken in a large bowl and mix well to make a rich marinade. Add the chicken and let it marinate for at least 30 minutes—longer does make it taste better. While the chicken marinates, work on the couscous.

To make the couscous, put the couscous, apricots, and cranberries in a medium bowl and pour the water over them, stirring with a fork to combine. Cover and let sit for 10 to 15 minutes, then uncover and fluff with a fork. Add the green onions and cilantro and drizzle with the lemon juice and olive oil. Season with the salt and pepper to taste and toss gently to combine. Set aside and keep warm.

To make the dish, heat a skillet or grill pan over medium heat and add the chicken. Brown the chicken on both sides, watching carefully as the spice mixture on the chicken can make it burn rather easily After browning both sides, turn the heat down to low and put a lid over the skillet, this will allow the chicken to almost steam, making for a very moist chicken breast. When the chicken is fully cooked, remove it from the heat and let it rest for 10 minutes and then slice against the grain. Serve with the couscous.

Yield: 4 to 6 servings

—Joanne Choi

Per serving (Chicken): 238 Cal.; 51 GI; 31g Prot.; 4g Carb.; 2g SFA; 6g MUFA; 2g PUFA; 0.1g Omega-3; 40mg Calc.; 434mg Sod.; 320mg Pot.; 2mg Iron; 0mg Phytoestrogen; 1g Fiber

Per serving (Couscous): 252 Cal.; 55 GI; 6g Prot.; 46g Carb.; 0.8g SFA; 4g MUFA; 0.7g PUFA; 0g Omega-3; 25mg Calc.; 10mg Sod.; 262mg Pot.; 1mg Iron; 0mg Phytoestrogen; 4g Fiber

CHICKEN:

1 teaspoon ground cinnamon

1 teaspoon ground cloves

1 teaspoon cayenne

1 teaspoon ground cumin

1 teaspoon fennel seeds

1 tablespoon sweet paprika

¾ teaspoon kosher salt

1 teaspoon brown sugar

Juice of ½ lemon

2 tablespoons olive oil

4 cloves of garlic, crushed

1½ to 2 pounds boneless skinless chicken breasts

COUSCOUS:

1 cup couscous

10 dried apricots

½ cup dried cranberries

1½ cups boiling water

2 green onions, green parts only, chopped

2 handfuls of chopped cilantro

Juice of ½ lemon

2 tablespoons extra-virgin olive oil

Kosher salt and freshly ground pepper

roasted chicken mediterranean

 This dish combines the flavors of Greece, Italy, and the South of France. A beautiful and robust dish, it is easy to prepare and perfect for a dinner party. You may simplify it or embellish it in many ways. Some delicious additions include artichokes, oven-cured tomatoes, and grilled Swiss chard. Chicken on the bone adds flavor, but you may choose to use boneless breast instead.

4 large chicken breasts, rib bone in

Kosher salt

Cracked peppercorns

Dried oregano

1 bay leaf

2 sprigs of thyme

1 bunch of Italian parsley, chopped

1 cup olive oil, divided

3 lemons

4 Idaho potatoes, unpeeled

2 cloves of garlic, halved

½ cup dry white wine

3 ounces sun-dried tomatoes

35 to 40 pitted Kalamata olives

2 sprigs of basil, thinly sliced

½ cup chicken broth

Place the chicken in a deep dish or bowl and season with the salt, cracked peppercorns, oregano, bay leaf, thyme, and half the chopped parsley. Pour ½ cup of the olive oil over top. Roll 2 of the lemons on the countertop back and forth to "loosen" up all the juices. Cut 1 lemon in half and squeeze all the juice onto the chicken, and then cut up the other lemon and add it to the bowl. Toss to mix well and coat the chicken. Marinate in the refrigerator for a couple of hours.

Wash the potatoes, dry them well, and cut each of them lengthwise into 8 wedges. Heat a few teaspoons of the remaining ½ cup of olive oil in a skillet over high heat. Add the potatoes and sauté until browned on all sides. Set aside.

Preheat the oven to 350°F.

Remove the chicken from the marinade and place in a heavy skillet and brown thoroughly over medium-high heat. Transfer the chicken to a heavy roasting pan large enough to hold the chicken and potatoes. Place the garlic and browned potatoes around the chicken and bake for about 20 minutes, or until the chicken is tender and tests done with a meat thermometer.

Place the chicken and potatoes on a serving platter. Place the roasting pan on the stove over medium heat, add the wine, and bring to a boil to deglaze the pan. Add the sun-dried tomatoes, olives, basil, and the remaining olive oil and mix well. Add the chicken broth, the juice of the remaining lemon, and the rest of the parsley and bring to a boil again. Season to taste and spoon over the chicken and serve.

Yield: 4 servings

—*Carrie Nahabedian*

Per serving: 716 Cal.; 55 GI; 35g Prot.; 59g Carb.; 6g SFA; 26g MUFA; 5g PUFA; 0.4g Omega-3; 191mg Calc.; 1,068mg Sod.; 2,254 mg Pot.; 10mg Iron; 0.012mg Phytoestrogen; 11g Fiber

whole roasted baby chicken and potato gnocchi with honey-glazed parsnips and young beets

 This recipe makes a truly tantalizing meal.

....

CHICKEN:

4 whole poussins (baby chickens)

Salt and cracked peppercorns

A few sprigs of thyme

¼ cup olive oil

4 teaspoons butter

½ cup dry white wine

VEGETABLES:

1 pound beets (golden, red, or Chioggia beets; baby or large)

2 tablespoons butter

2 parsnips, peeled and cut into preferred shape

2 tablespoons honey

GNOCCHI:

2 tablespoons butter

16 potato gnocchi

Buy fresh baby chickens at a specialty butcher shop such as Fox & Obel. Have the butcher truss them for you if possible. If not, chop the wing bones off at the center joint and trim the neck and skin. Truss by using string and tie starting with the string around the feet and crossing down and over the wings and then to the neck. Knot and cut.

Season the chickens with salt and cracked peppercorns and stuff the insides with a few sprigs of thyme.

Preheat the oven to 350°F.

Heat the olive oil in a large skillet over medium-high heat. Pat the chickens dry and place them in the skillet and sauté until browned completely on all sides. Place the chickens in a roasting pan and dab a pat of butter on top of each bird. Place in the oven and roast for 25 minutes, or until a meat thermometer reaches 170°F. Remove from the oven, deglaze the pan with the wine, and reserve the roasting juices. Let the birds cool, and then remove the meat from the bones. The meat can be refrigerated for 4 days for future use if desired.

To make the vegetables, place the beets in a saucepan filled with cold water and cook over medium-high heat until a knife can be easily inserted into the center of the beets. Cool under running cold water and trim the beets and peel off their skins. (When cleaning red beets, it is advised to wear plastic gloves since they easily stain your hands.) Halve the beets or cut them into wedges, depending on the size. Set aside. The beets can be stored in the refrigerator for up to 4 days.

Preheat the oven to 350°F.

Heat the butter in a heavy oven-proof skillet over medium-high heat. Add the parsnips and sauté until tender. Drizzle the parsnips with the honey, place in the oven, and roast until they are glazed and caramelized. Set aside.

To prepare the gnocchi, heat the butter in a heavy skillet over medium-high heat. Add the gnocchi and sauté until cooked through. Set aside.

To serve, preheat the oven to 200°F. Place the chicken on a serving platter and place the gnocchi around the chicken. Top with the glazed parsnips and beets and place in the oven for a few minutes to heat through. Remove from the oven and drizzle with a good extra-virgin olive oil or with the pan juices from roasting the birds.

Yield: 4 servings

—*Carrie Nahabedian*

Per serving: 552 Cal.; 74 GI; 40g Prot.; 69g Carb.; 5g SFA; 4g MUFA; 2g PUFA; 0.2g Omega-3; 93mg Calc.; 1,060mg Sod.; 1,108mg Pot.; 4mg Iron; 0mg Phytoestrogen; 8g Fiber

grandma greenwood's roasted sunday chicken

 Braising is a wonderful way to cook meats in the oven while you are at church, because you don't need to worry about overcooking or burning your dinner. The result is a dish that is "fork tender," as chefs call it. Will Greenwood always loved Sundays, because when he and his family got home from church, they would always have a wonderful feast, which was part of their southern heritage. They loved the "warmed-overs" too, as braised meats always reheat well and are, in fact, sometimes even better the next day. This dish is not only a wonderful meal, it is also very healthy and a great way to get the kids to eat their vegetables too! (If fresh herbs aren't available, substitute with 1½ teaspoons of poultry seasoning.)

1 (4½ to 5-pound) roasting chicken

2 pounds fingerling potatoes

1 pound peeled baby carrots

1 pound turnips, peeled and halved

1 pound rutabaga, peeled and cut into large dice

1 head of cabbage, quartered and cored

1 pound parsnips, peeled and cut into large dice

1 pound pearl onions, peeled

2 heads of garlic, halved crosswise to expose the individual cloves of garlic

Preheat the oven to 320°F.

Remove the inside pouch and neck from the chicken and reserve for another use. Wash the chicken well in cold water and pat dry. Place it in a large roasting pan and arrange the vegetables around the chicken. Add the herbs and set aside. (If using poultry seasoning instead of fresh herbs, add it in the next step.)

Pour the broth into a saucepan and place over medium heat. Add the onion soup powder and poultry seasoning if you are using it instead of the fresh herbs. Stir and cook until dissolved, and then pour the mixture into the roasting pan. Cover the pan, place it in the oven, and braise for 1½ to 2 hours, or until a leg easily pulls away from the joint.

When done, remove from the oven and transfer the chicken to a large serving platter and arrange the vegetables around it. Pour the pan juices into a pitcher or fat separator, and when the fat rises to the top, pour the defatted juices into a saucepan and bring to a simmer on the stove. Add the flour, a little at a time, and stir until you have a sauce that is thickened to your taste. Pour the sauce into a gravy boat and serve on the side.

Yield: 6 servings (plus leftovers)

—Will Greenwood

Per serving: 789 Cal.; 72 GI; 55g Prot.; 121g Carb.; 3g SFA; 4g MUFA; 3g PUFA; 0.4g Omega-3; 417mg Calc.; 1,332mg Sod.; 3,580mg Pot.; 9mg Iron; 0mg Phytoestrogen; 27g Fiber

2 sprigs of thyme

2 sprigs of oregano

2 sprigs of rosemary

4 cups chicken broth

1 pouch Lipton onion soup

All-purpose flour

delectable sweet-and-sour tofu

 Tofu, a heart-healthy food made from soybeans, is very high in protein and is a good source of iron, omega-3 fatty acids (the heart-healthy fats), phosphorus, copper, calcium, and magnesium. If you think you don't like tofu, you probably just haven't had it prepared the right way! This dish is delicious served with rice and green beans.

1 pound extra-firm tofu

1 tablespoon vegetable or peanut oil

SAUCE:

Juice and zest of 1 lime

¼ cup freshly squeezed orange juice

½ teaspoon lemon pepper seasoning

1 tablespoon reduced-sodium soy sauce

1 tablespoon Asian sweet chili sauce (or 1 tablespoon orange marmalade and 1/8 teaspoon red pepper flakes)

Drain the tofu, wrap it in a clean dishcloth, and let it rest for at least 10 minutes and up to 2 hours to remove the water.

Cut the tofu crosswise into 3 equal rectangles, and then cut each rectangle into 4 long strips.

To make the sauce, in a mixing bowl, combine the lime juice and zest, orange juice, lemon pepper seasoning, soy sauce, and chili sauce and mix well. Set aside.

Heat the oil in a large non-stick skillet over medium to medium-high heat until the oil is very hot. Add the tofu strips in a single layer and let them cook for about 4 minutes on each side, until they are medium brown on the top and bottom. When the tofu is browned, add the sauce and let it boil down for about 2 minutes, until the sauce is thick. Remove from the heat and serve immediately.

Yield: 4 servings

—Aviva Goldfarb

Variation: Add ½ teaspoon of Asian Chili Garlic Sauce to the marinade.

Per serving: 154 Cal.; 34 GI; 12g Prot.; 7g Carb.; 1g SFA; 6g MUFA; 2g PUFA; 0.006g Omega-3; 212mg Calc.; 243mg Sod.; 227mg Pot.; 2mg Iron; 26mg Phytoestrogen; 2g Fiber

grilled marinated tempeh

 Fire up the grill and lower your hot flashes as you enjoy this healthy way to barbeque.

To prepare the marinade, combine the lemon juice, olive oil, thyme, and pepper to taste in a small bowl; set aside. Cut the tempeh into 4 slices. Using a steamer, steam the tempeh for 15 minutes. Place the tempeh and onions in a 2-quart casserole and pour the marinade over them. Refrigerate for at least 4 hours.

Preheat the oven to 400°F.

Cover the casserole dish and bake for 30 to 35 minutes (or grill, basting frequently with the marinade). Garnish with lettuce and tomato if desired. Serve hot on hamburger rolls.

Yield: 4 servings

—Dr. Mache's Kitchen

Per serving: 471 Cal.; 55 GI; 27g Prot.; 35g Carb.; 5g SFA; 14g MUFA; 6g PUFA; 0.37g Omega-3; 191mg Calc.; 220mg Sod.; 762mg Pot.; 4mg Iron; 50mg Phytoestrogen; 8 g Fiber

¼ cup lemon juice

¼ cup olive oil

¼ teaspoon dried thyme

Pepper

16 ounces tempeh

1 large onion, sliced into rings

Lettuce and tomato slices for garnish (optional)

4 whole-wheat hamburger rolls

eggplant-tofu lasagna (no noodles)

 This is a wonderful vegetarian lasagna that uses eggplant instead of pasta. It's easy to make and delicious. Enjoy!

1 tablespoon olive oil or oil spray

1 large eggplant, peeled and cut into ¼-inch strips

3 cups pasta sauce (or you could make your own), divided

1 (1-pound) brick of extra-firm tofu, sliced

4 tomatoes, sliced

1 bunch of basil, leaves separated

1 (1-pound) package of shredded mozzarella cheese

½ pound grated Parmesan cheese

Preheat the oven to 350°F. Grease a cookie sheet and a 4 by 4-inch baking dish with the olive oil or cooking spray.

Place the eggplant strips on the greased cookie sheet and bake for 10 minutes, or until tender. Set aside.

Spoon ¾ cup of the pasta sauce into the greased baking dish and place one-third of the eggplant strips (in place of noodles) as the first layer of the lasagna. Add one-third of the tofu slices in another layer, followed by one-third of the sliced tomatoes and then one-third of the basil leaves. Spoon another ¾ cup of the pasta sauce over the basil, followed by one-third of the mozzarella and parmesan cheeses. Repeat the same layers twice more, ending with a layer of pasta sauce topped with the cheeses. Place in the oven and bake for 45 minutes. Serve immediately.

Yield: 4 servings

—*Catherine D'Amato*

Per serving: 542 Cal.; 50 GI; 43g Prot.; 35g Carb.; 12g SFA; 12g MUFA; 1g PUFA; 0.2g Omega-3; 1,071mg Calc.; 1,333mg Sod.; 1,176mg Pot.; 5mg Iron; 34mg Phytoestrogen; 9g Fiber

charcoal-grilled seitan skewers

This recipe is known as "Seitan Chimichurris" at the Candle Café and Candle 79 restaurant in New York City, where it is one of the restaurant's all-time favorites. They have been known to ship these appetizers to friends and customers on the West Coast who have called in need of a fix. These seitan skewers freeze very well and are great to have on hand to serve as appetizers, snacks, or an entrée.

To prepare the marinade, put the lemon juice, olive oil garlic, agave nectar, salt, parsley, and cilantro in a food processor and blend on high speed until well combined.

To prepare the seitan skewers, put 4 pieces of seitan on each of 12 metal skewers and place them in a large non-reactive bowl or baking dish. Pour the marinade over them and let them marinate for at least 1 hour or overnight.

Prepare a charcoal, gas, or stove-top grill. Remove the seitan skewers from the marinade and pour the marinade into a sauce boat. Grill the skewers over medium-high heat until well-browned, about 5 to 7 minutes per side. Serve immediately with the citrus-herb sauce on the side.

Yield: 6 servings (12 skewers)

—Benay Vynerib

Per serving (about 2 tablespoons) (Marinade): 169 Cal.; 30 Gl; 0.2g Prot.; 2g Carb.; 2g SFA; 13g MUFA; 2g PUFA; 0.1g Omega-3; 19mg Calc.; 199mg Sod.; 50mg Pot.; 0.5mg Iron; 0mg Phytoestrogen; 0.5g Fiber

Per serving (Seitan skewers): 518 Cal.; 69 Gl; 104g Prot.; 20g Carb.; 0.3g SFA; 0.2g MUFA; 1g PUFA; 0.06g Omega-3; 201mg Calc.; 386mg Sod.; 156mg Pot.; 7mg Iron; 0.05mg Phytoestrogen; 1g Fiber

MARINADE:

1 cup fresh lemon juice

1 cup olive oil

2 cloves of garlic, minced

¼ cup agave nectar

1 teaspoon salt

½ cup finely chopped fresh parsley

1 cup finely chopped cilantro

1½ pounds seitan, cut into 1½-inch pieces

tofu cacciatore

 This is a flavorful dish that tastes delicious as an entrée or the next day as a side dish. Add a salad and you've got a rich isoflavone dish that will appeal to everyone in the family. This recipe comes with kudos to Mark Stanzler, former sous-chef at the Meridian Hotel in Boston.

CAJUN SEASONING:

4 tablespoons chili powder

3 tablespoons paprika

1½ tablespoons garlic powder

1 tablespoon kosher salt

1 tablespoon ground pepper

CACCIATORE:

Olive oil

8 cloves of garlic, minced

Kosher salt

Freshly ground pepper

2 Vidalia onions, chopped

2 green bell peppers, chopped

1 red bell pepper, chopped

Italian seasoning

2 pounds tofu, cut into ½-inch sheets

Cajun seasoning (above)

Couple of splashes of dry red wine

Dash of Worcestershire sauce (optional)

To make the Cajun seasoning, combine all the seasoning ingredients in small bowl and mix well. Set aside.

To make the cacciatore, heat a generous amount of olive oil in a large saucepan over medium-high heat. Add the garlic and sauté for 1 minute. Add a shake of kosher salt and pepper and the onions and sauté for another 1 to 2 minutes, and then add the bell peppers and some Italian seasoning and sauté for a few more minutes. Remove from the heat and spoon into a large casserole, leaving whatever olive oil is left in the saucepan.

Preheat the oven to 375°F.

Add more olive oil to the saucepan and put it back on the stove over medium-high heat. Coat the tofu sheets with the Cajun seasoning and fry them for a few minutes on each side until they are crispy. As the tofu is fried, add it to the casserole with the onion mixture and toss the onion mixture over the tofu. Splash with the wine and the Worcestershire sauce if using. Cover with the tomato-basil and spicy red pepper sauces and place over medium heat. When it begins to bubble, use a sturdy spatula to lift up the tofu so the mixture can get underneath. Lower the heat to medium and crumble the feta cheese over top. Liberally sprinkle the Parmesan cheese, and then a little Italian seasoning, over top, finishing with a shake or two of paprika. Bake in the oven for 35 to 40 minutes, until bubbling and slightly crispy brown.

Cook the pasta al dente according to the package instructions. Drain, return to the saucepan, and cover with a little olive oil, Parmesan cheese, and the chopped parsley. Serve the tofu cacciatore over the pasta with a loaf of crusty bread if you like.

Yield: 8 to 10 servings

—*Ben Schwendener*

Per serving: 665 Cal.; 44 GI; 36g Prot.; 79g Carb.; 6g SFA; 16g MUFA; 3g PUFA; 0.2g Omega-3; 543mg Calc.; 612mg Sod.; 827mg Pot.; 8mg Iron; 47mg Phytoestrogen; 11g Fiber

1 (26-ounce) jar tomato-basil sauce

¼ to ½ cup spicy red pepper sauce

½ pound feta cheese

Grated Parmesan cheese (and/or Romano and Asiago cheeses)

Dash of paprika

2 (1-pound) packages of pasta

1 cup chopped parsley

cold tofu with cilantro, green onions, and soy sesame sauce

 This simple, nutritious tofu dish is a deliciously healthy meat substitute for lunch or dinner. And it's great for hot flashes and building strong bones.

1 (1-pound) package soft tofu (sometimes called silken tofu)

1 tablespoon soy sauce

1 tablespoon sesame oil

3 tablespoons chopped green onions

2 tablespoons chopped cilantro

Carefully slice the tofu into even pieces (about ½ inch thick). Lay them flat on a plate.

In a small bowl, combine the soy sauce and sesame oil and drizzle a little over top of each tofu slice. Then sprinkle the tofu with the green onions and cilantro and serve.

Yield: 4 to 6 servings

—Joanne Choi

Per serving: 83 Cal.;19 GI; 6.5g Prot.; 3g Carb.; 1g SFA; 2g MUFA; 2g PUFA; 0.1g Omega-3; 32mg Calc.; 213mg Sod.; 194mg Pot.; 1mg Iron; 26mg Phytoestrogen; 0g Fiber

maine wild blueberry granola french toast

 This dish is a great way to start off your day!

Preheat the oven to 450°F.

To make the batter, whip the egg whites until they form a soft peak, adding the sugar only at the end. In a separate bowl, whisk the yolks and the milk together. Gently fold one-third of the whites into the yolk mixture. Fold the remaining whites into the mixture in two separate stages.

To make the French toast, dip the toast slices into the batter to coat evenly. Sprinkle the tops evenly with the granola. Heat the butter in an oven-proof skillet over medium-high heat. Place the slices of toast in the skillet and cook for 4 to 5 minutes, until golden brown on the bottom, and then flip the toast slices over and place the pan in the oven for 3 to 4 minutes to finish cooking. Serve immediately with your favorite topping.

Yield: 2 servings

—Chef Jonathan Cartwright

Per serving: 468 Cal.; 62 GI; 15g Prot.; 67g Carb.; 3g SFA; 8g MUFA; 4g PUFA; 0.7g Omega-3; 115mg Calc.; 334mg Sod.; 310mg Pot.; 3mg Iron; 0.8mg Phytoestrogen; 5g Fiber

BATTER:

2 eggs, separated

2 tablespoons sugar

¼ cup milk

FRENCH TOAST:

2 (1-inch-thick) slices of brioche toast

1 cup Wild Maine Blueberry Granola, coarsely ground

2 tablespoons butter

whole-grain pancakes

 This healthy recipe will soon become one of your favorites. The pancakes are light and fluffy and you can add blueberries or other fruits to suit your own unique taste.

½ cup whole-wheat flour

¼ cup sifted all-purpose flour

2 scoops soy protein powder

2 teaspoons non-aluminum baking powder

¼ teaspoon salt

1 1/3 cups soymilk (or water)

2 tablespoons oil

Cooking spray

Mix together the flours, soy protein powder, baking powder, and salt in a medium bowl. Add the soymilk and oil and stir just until blended. Spray a large skillet or griddle with cooking spray and heat over medium-high heat until hot enough to evaporate a drop of water immediately upon contact.

Spoon the batter by ¼ cup measures onto the hot skillet or griddle. Cook until evenly covered with bubbles, about 2 minutes. Using a spatula, carefully turn over and cook for 1 to 2 minutes more, until lightly browned. Repeat with the remaining batter. Spray the griddle or skillet again with cooking spray every time after making 2 pancakes.

Yield: 4 servings (2 pancakes per serving)

—*Dr. Mache's Kitchen*

Tip: If you're looking for a simpler way to start your day, just reach into the food pantry and pull out your favorite pancake mix and substitute soymilk in equal measure for the milk or water you would normally use.

Per serving: 237 Cal.; 62 GI; 9g Prot.; 32g Carb.; 1g SFA; 5g MUFA; 3g PUFA; 1g Omega-3; 318mg Calc.; 488mg Sod.; 312mg Pot.; 4mg Iron; 9mg Phytoestrogen; 3g Fiber

dewberry's black fingers egg scramble

 This slightly spicy, rich breakfast scramble has more going for it than meets the eye. A delicious mix of eggs cooked with fingerling potatoes, black beans, garlic, and onions will start the day out right. You can top the finished scramble with diced tomatoes and avocado if you have them lying in wait. Enjoy!

In a microwave-safe bowl, add a few drops of water. If your potatoes are thick, you will need to prick them with a fork before cooking. Place the potatoes in the bowl, cover with plastic wrap, and cook for 3 to 4 minutes on high, or until the potatoes are tender. Slice them in half and set aside.

In a stainless steel saucepan, heat the olive oil over medium heat. Add the onions and sauté for 3 minutes. Add the potatoes and sauté for 1 minute longer. Add the garlic and sauté for another minute. Add the beans and sauté for 2 minutes more.

Break the eggs into a small bowl and add the cumin and salt and pepper to taste and beat with a fork. Add to the bean mixture and cook for about 1 minute or more to your desired consistency.

Add as much Tabasco sauce as you like and top with the diced tomato and avocado if desired.

Yield: 1 serving

—Jeffrey Parker

Per serving: 477 Cal.; 54 GI; 21g Prot.; 62g Carb.; 4g SFA; 8g MUFA; 2g PUFA; 0.2g Omega-3; 185mg Calc.; 914mg Sod.; 1,885mg Pot.; 7mg Iron; 0.19mg Phytoestrogen; 10g Fiber

5 or 6 small fingerling potatoes

1 teaspoon extra-virgin olive oil

1 to 2 tablespoons diced white onion

1 clove of garlic, minced

¼ to 1/3 cup canned black beans

2 eggs

½ teaspoon ground cumin

Salt and pepper

2 to 20 dashes Tabasco sauce

Diced tomato (optional)

Diced avocado (optional)

eggs in the nest

This recipe from the *Low GI Family Cookbook* makes a lovely lazy weekend breakfast or brunch. Prepare double the quantity for four people—or for seconds. Use omega 3 eggs for less saturated fat, or egg whites

2 slices whole-grain bread

Olive oil cooking spray

1 teaspoon olive oil margarine

1½ ounces button mushrooms (about 4), stems trimmed, sliced

3 large (not baby) spinach leaves, washed and chopped

Freshly ground pepper

2 eggs

1 tablespoon coarsely grated reduced-fat Cheddar cheese

Preheat the oven to 350°F.

Cut the crusts off the bread. Spray both sides of each slice lightly with oil. Press the bread slices firmly into two 1/3-cup capacity non-stick muffin tins. Set aside.

Heat the margarine in a non-stick frying pan over medium-high heat until sizzling. Add the mushrooms and cook, stirring often, for 4 to 5 minutes, or until tender. Add the spinach and cook, stirring, for 1 to 2 minutes, or until wilted. Remove from the heat and season with pepper to taste.

Spoon half the mushroom mixture over each of the muffin cups of bread and press lightly. Crack an egg into a small dish and then slide it on top of the mushrooms. Repeat with the remaining egg. Sprinkle with the cheese. Bake for 15 minutes (for a softly set yolk), 20 minutes (for a hard-cooked yolk), or until the egg is cooked to your liking. Serve warm or at room temperature.

Yield: 2 servings

—The University of Sydney Glycemic Index and GI Database

Per serving: 175 Cal.; 67 GI; 12g Prot.; 13g Carb.; 2g SFA; 3g MUFA; 1g PUFA; 0.1g Omega-3; 96mg Calc.; 257mg Sod.; 288mg Pot.; 2mg Iron; 0mg Phytoestrogen; 2.5 g Fiber

green bean bits with crispy garlic

 Fresh from your garden or a local market, green beans are a refreshing vegetable side dish any time of year. Paired with crispy garlic and a mild olive oil, you will be reaching for a guilt-free second helping!

Cut the green beans into ¾-inch bits. The easiest way to do this is to grab a handful, line them up, and slice through the bunch.

Heat the oil in a skillet over medium-high heat. Add the garlic and a pinch of salt and sauté very carefully, until the garlic is golden; be very careful not to let it burn. When the garlic is golden, add the bean bits and sauté until the beans are tender and slightly blistered, about 5 minutes. Serve and enjoy!

Yield: 5 servings

—*Joanne Choi*

Per serving: 82 Cal.; 60 GI; 2g Prot.; 8g Carb.; 0.5g SFA; 3g MUFA; 1.5g PUFA; 0.5g Omega-3; 40mg Calc.; 242mg Sod.; 204mg Pot.; 1mg Iron; 0mg Phytoestrogen; 3g Fiber

1 pound fresh green beans (or French green beans)

5 to 6 cloves of garlic, thinly sliced

2 tablespoons mild-flavored oil (such as canola oil, or even olive oil)

Salt and pepper

byaldi confit and crispy artichokes with saffron-tomato nage

 A spin on the traditional ratatouille, this recipe is hearty for body and soul.

BYALDI CONFIT:

3 tablespoons olive oil, plus more for seasoning

3 red onions, thinly sliced

Salt and pepper

4 zucchinis, sliced into 1/8-inch-thick rounds

4 Japanese eggplants, sliced into 1/8-inch-thick rounds

4 yellow summer squash, sliced into 1/8-inch-thick rounds

5 Roma tomatoes, sliced into 1/8-inch-thick rounds

CRISPY ARTICHOKES:

3 large artichokes, peeled, choked, and soaked in lemon water

Salt

4 cups or more olive oil

¼ teaspoon dried thyme

SAFFRON-TOMATO NAGE:

2 tablespoons olive oil

1 white onion, chopped

2 cloves of garlic, chopped

To make the byaldi confit, preheat the oven to 275°F. Heat the 3 tablespoons of olive oil in a skillet over medium heat. Add the onions and cook slowly, stirring occasionally, until caramelized (well browned). Season with salt and pepper and spread evenly onto a rimmed baking sheet. Arrange alternating slices of the vegetables, 1 slice each of zucchini, eggplant, squash, and tomato, in rows over the onions, overlapping so that ¼ inch of each slice is exposed. Season with salt and olive oil and cover with foil. Bake in the oven for 2 hours. Remove from the oven, take off the foil, and set aside.

To make the artichokes, preheat the oven to 300°F. Drain the artichokes, place them in a baking dish, and season them with salt. Pour enough olive oil over the artichokes to submerge them, and then stir in the thyme. Cover and bake for 45 minutes, or until fork tender. When cooked, remove the artichokes from the baking dish and let drain on paper towels. (Reserve a few teaspoons of the olive oil.) When cool enough to handle, slice the artichokes thinly. Heat the reserved olive oil in a skillet over high heat, add the artichoke slices, and fry until golden brown. Set aside.

To make the saffron-tomato nage, heat the olive oil in a saucepan over medium-high heat. Add the onion, garlic, and shallots and sauté until the vegetables are tender. Add the tomatoes, saffron, wine, and broth and bring to a simmer. Cook uncovered until the sauce has reduced by one-third. Stir in the butter and strain through a chinois strainer into a sauce boat.

To serve, preheat the broiler, place the byaldi confit underneath, and broil until the vegetables are lightly browned. Serve the byaldi confit and the crispy artichokes with the saffron-tomato nage on the side.

Yield: 10 servings

—Chef Neal Fraser

Per serving: 201 Cal.; 60 GI; 6g Prot.; 28g Carb.; 3g SFA; 4g MUFA; 1g PUFA; 0.1g Omega-3; 70mg Calc.; 391mg Sod.; 1,194mg Pot.; 2mg Iron; 0mg Phytoestrogen; 12g Fiber

2 shallots, chopped

4 Roma tomatoes, chopped

Pinch of saffron

½ cup white wine

2 cups vegetable broth or water

4 tablespoons butter (½ stick)

oven-roasted artichokes with garlic and anchovies

 This is an extraordinary and excellent way to prepare artichokes. Serve alone as a main course, or as an appetizer.

4 large artichokes

Juice of ¼ lemon

1 teaspoon salt

2 teaspoons anchovy paste (or 4 small fillets, scraped and minced)

Pinch of salt

2 shallots, minced

4 cloves of garlic, minced

1 cup fresh bread crumbs (or panko)

3 tablespoons chopped parsley

4 tablespoons olive oil

1 lemon, cut into 4 wedges

Preheat the oven to 375°F.

Trim the stems from the bottom of the artichokes so that they will sit up on a plate. Reserve the stems. Bring 2 to 3 quarts of water to a boil in a large saucepan. Add the artichokes, their stems, the lemon juice, and 1 teaspoon of salt and cook at a rolling boil for 8 to 10 minutes, or until they are three-quarters cooked. Take the artichokes and stems out of the water with a slotted spoon and let them drain and cool on a cookie sheet.

When the artichokes are cool enough to handle, spread the leaves out and remove and discard the inner leaves. Using a small teaspoon, scrape out the inner "chokes" and discard them. Set the artichokes aside. Cut the stems up into a small dice and place them in a small bowl. Add the anchovy paste (or anchovies), pinch of salt, shallots, garlic, bread crumbs, parsley, and salt and pepper to taste to the bowl and toss lightly to combine.

Place the artichokes in a shallow baking dish so they sit with the leaves facing up. Lightly fill the cavity of each with 2 to 3 tablespoons of the bread crumb filling. Spread the leaves out slightly and sprinkle the remaining filling in between the leaves. Drizzle each artichoke with 1 tablespoon of olive oil and a few drops of lemon juice. Fill the bottom of the baking dish with ¼ inch of water.

Place the artichokes in the oven and bake for 20 to 30 minutes, or until the artichokes are warm and the bread crumbs are golden brown and toasted on the top. Serve hot from the oven as a main dish with lemon wedges on the side.

Yield: 4 servings

—Gordon Hamersley

Per serving: 320 Cal.; 65 GI; 8g Prot.; 40g Carb.; 2g SFA; 10g MUFA; 2g PUFA; 0.2g Omega-3; 96mg Calc.; 1,054mg Sod.; 523mg Pot.; 3mg Iron; 0.3mg Phytoestrogen; 12g Fiber

> ⅅo you remember when your mother used to say . . .
> "Eat your vegetables, they're good, and they're good for you"? She was right! To stay well, eat a lot of them; more as you grow older. If you're physically active, you may be able to eat even more and not gain weight. Eating vegetables daily helps prevent certain diseases, including some cancers, and helps control your weight.

meatless sloppy joes

Enjoy this healthy approach to an American classic. It's easy to make and good for you. Vegetable protein can be used as a substitute for many meat dishes.

1 cup textured vegetable protein

1 cup boiling water

1 (16-ounce) can sloppy Joe sauce

4 whole-wheat hamburger rolls

Place the textured vegetable protein in a medium saucepan and pour the boiling water over it to rehydrate. Stir and let stand for 5 to 10 minutes. Stir in the sloppy Joe sauce and cook over medium heat for 3 to 4 minutes, or until thoroughly heated. Spoon the mixture onto 4 buns and serve.

Yield: 4 servings

—*Dr. Mache's Kitchen*

Per serving: 298 Cal.; 74 GI; 19g Prot.; 46g Carb.; 1g SFA; 2g MUFA; 2g PUFA; 0.15g Omega-3; 137mg Calc.; 766mg Sod.; 1,062mg Pot.; 5mg Iron; 37mg Phytoestrogen; 8g Fiber

Savor your food
Eat slowly and experience your food; don't eat while watching TV and don't jump up immediately from the table when finished eating; relax a moment and digest.

baked eggplant

Eggplant is a very healthy vegetable: It's low in calories, fat, and cholesterol, and it's a good source of vitamin K, thiamin, vitamin B6, folate, and manganese, as well as dietary fiber. This recipe makes a wonderful vegetarian meal straight from Bubbie's kitchen.

Preheat the oven to 350°F.

Place the eggplant chunks in a saucepan with the boiling water and salt and boil for 5 to 10 minutes, or until tender. Drain and set aside.

Heat the oil in a saucepan over medium-high heat. Add the onions and garlic and sauté until golden brown. Add the eggplant, egg, and bread crumbs and season to taste with salt and pepper.

Transfer the eggplant mixture to an 8-inch square baking pan and bake for 15 to 20 minutes, until brown. (You can sprinkle some bread crumbs over top before baking if you wish.)

Yield: 4 servings

—Bubbie's Kitchen

Per serving: 198 Cal.; 61 GI; 6g Prot.; 26g Carb.; 1g SFA; 5g MUFA; 2g PUFA; 0.6g Omega-3; 64mg Calc.; 375mg Sod.; 770mg Pot.; 1mg Iron; 0.073mg Phytoestrogen; 11g Fiber

2 medium eggplants, peeled and cut into 2-inch chunks

3 cups boiling water

Pinch of salt

2 tablespoons vegetable oil

2 medium onions, chopped

1 clove of garlic, minced

1 large egg, beaten

¼ cup bread crumbs

Salt and pepper

lemon and mint marinated roast leg of lamb with a ragout of flageolet beans, oven-cured tomatoes, garlic confit, and kalamata olives

 Roasted lamb is the typical meat choice for spring dinners, and this roast lamb dish is exceptionally delicious. All will enjoy its sweet, rich flavor. (The tomatoes and garlic confit can be prepared ahead of time.)

TOMATOES:

12 Roma tomatoes, cored and halved lengthwise

Salt and pepper

1 cup olive oil

3 sprigs of thyme

GARLIC CONFIT:

4 heads of garlic, cloves separated and peeled

1 cup olive oil, plus more for drizzling

FLAGEOLETS:

1 (4-ounce) slab of bacon, sliced and then cut into ¼-inch pieces (optional)

1 medium onion, finely chopped

1 sprig of thyme

1 bunch of parsley

1 bay leaf

2 pounds flageolets, rinsed and drained

4 cups chicken broth, fresh or canned

To prepare the tomatoes, preheat the oven to 400°F, leave on for 2 hours, and then turn the heat off.

Place the tomatoes, cut side up, on the rack of a baking pan. Season generously with salt and pepper. Drizzle the tomatoes with the olive oil and add the sprigs of thyme. Place the tomatoes in the oven overnight to cure and dry. Remove the tomatoes from the oven in the morning. They should be slightly caramelized and semi-dry, but still plump. If the desired effect is not achieved overnight, you can turn the oven back on and dry the tomatoes out for no more than 30 minutes. The tomatoes can be prepared up to 3 days in advance and kept in the refrigerator.

To make the garlic confit, preheat the oven to 325°F.

Set aside 8 cloves of the garlic and place the remaining cloves in a baking dish and cover with 1 cup of olive oil. Bake in the oven until the garlic cloves are soft but still firm enough to keep their shape. Remove from the oven and let cool in the oil. This can be done up to a week in advance and the garlic can be stored in the refrigerator.

To make the flageolets, preheat the oven to 350°F.

Place the bacon (if using) in a heavy casserole or deep 3-quart saucepan and cook over high heat to render the bacon fat. (If not using the bacon, heat 3 tablespoons of olive oil instead.) Add the onions and sauté until tender. Add 4 of the uncooked garlic cloves, the sprig of thyme, the parsley, and the bay leaf. Stir in the flageolets and coat them thoroughly. Add a nice drizzle of olive oil, and then pour in the chicken broth to cover the flageolets. Bring to a boil and then place in the oven covered with either buttered parchment paper or a lid. Cook very slowly and carefully for about 1 hour, until the flageolets are firm but tender and cooked through. Do not overcook! Check the flageolets at least twice during cooking and stir them gently. Remove from the oven and let cool in the juice. (The juice will become the sauce.)

To make the lamb, preheat the oven to 375°F. With a sharp knife, remove the thick excess of fat from the lamb and season with the kosher salt and cracked peppercorns, and then rub it with olive oil. Mince 2 of the uncooked garlic cloves and place the leg of lamb in a heavy roasting pan and rub it with half the torn mint and the minced garlic. Thinly slice the remaining 2 cloves of uncooked garlic. With the tip of a paring knife, gently "jab" the lamb in various spots and place a sliver of garlic in each slit. This adds an added boost of flavor!

Roll the lemons on your countertop (this produces the maximum juice) and cut them in half and squeeze the juice over the top of the lamb and rub it in. Place in the oven and roast to your desired doneness. Medium-rare to medium will take about 90 minutes. Baste the lamb many times during roasting to add flavor and moistness.

(continued on next page)

LAMB:

1 semi-boneless leg of lamb (inner thigh bone removed and leg tied with twine)

Kosher salt and cracked peppercorns

Olive oil

2 bunches of mint, torn

2 lemons

75 pitted Kalamata olives, rinsed and halved lengthwise

To serve, place the lamb on a cutting board and let rest for 10 minutes. Slice the lamb and place on a serving platter or individual plates. Place the oven-cured tomatoes around the lamb and sprinkle with the olives. With a slotted spoon, spoon the flageolets over the meat. Heat the juice quickly over medium-high heat, add the remaining torn mint and infuse for a couple of minutes. Spoon the garlic confit over top of the flageolets and then drizzle with the mint jus.

The leg will serve 8 very generously and the remainder makes a great meal the next day.

Yield: 8 to 12 servings

—Carrie Nahabedian

Per serving: 918 Cal.; 32 GI; 46g Prot.; 59g Carb.; 7g SFA; 39g MUFA; 6g PUFA; 0.8g Omega-3; 169mg Calc.; 687mg Sod.; 1,485mg Pot.; 10mg Iron; 0.89mg Phytoestrogen; 17g Fiber

Desserts

apples with raisins

 This is a homey dessert that's easy to make and difficult to resist. However, it is high in saturated fat.

¼ cup golden raisins

1 teaspoon ground cinnamon

½ teaspoon ground ginger

Pinch of ground cumin

2 tablespoons butter

4 apples

5 tablespoons moscato dessert wine

Preheat oven to 325°F. Lightly grease a baking dish with a small amount of butter.

Soak the raisins in hot water for about 10 minutes to rehydrate. Drain the raisins, and then combine them in a small bowl with the cinnamon, ginger, and cumin. Set aside.

Core the apples, fill the cavity with the raisin mixture, and place the apples in the greased baking dish. Dot the apples with the butter and sprinkle with the wine and bake for 30 minutes. Remove from the oven and let cool slightly before serving.

Yield: 4 servings

—*Karen's Cucina*

Per serving: 205 Cal.; 46 GI; 1g Prot.; 35g Carb.; 4g SFA; 1g MUFA; 0g PUFA; 0.04g Omega-3; 27mg Calc.; 46mg Sod.; 289mg Pot.; 0.5mg Iron; 0.032mg Phytoestrogen; 5g Fiber

stuffed pears

This special dessert is easy to make and absolutely delicious, and it is healthy and low in fat. The wine combined with the sweetness of the pears makes a scrumptious dish.

Preheat oven to 400°F. Lightly grease a baking dish with a small amount of butter.

Combine the almonds and sugar in a small bowl and mix well. Place each pear half in the greased baking dish so that they fit snugly together. Stuff each pear half with the sugar-nut mixture, and then pour a little of the marsala on top of each pear. Bake uncovered for 10 minutes. Serve warm.

Yield: 4 servings

—*Karen's Cucina*

Per serving: 190 Cal.; 37 GI; 4g Prot.; 24g Carb.; 1g SFA; 5g MUFA; 2g PUFA; 0g Omega-3; 59mg Calc.; 2mg Sod.; 261mg Pot.; 1mg Iron; 0mg Phytoestrogen; 5g Fiber

½ cup sliced almonds, toasted and finely chopped

1 tablespoon confectioners' sugar

2 large ripe pears, halved and cored

3 tablespoons dry marsala wine

strawberries with ricotta topping

 Fresh strawberries with some sweetened ricotta on top really tastes like summer to me. This recipe is high in saturated fat.

¼ cup coarsely chopped walnuts

¼ cup white chocolate chunks

1 (15-ounce) package ricotta cheese (non-fat), crumbled

1 (4-ounce) package of light cream cheese

¼ cup sugar

2 tablespoons vanilla extract

Fresh strawberries

Place the walnuts and chocolate in a food processor and pulse until the mixture becomes coarse in texture. Place the cheeses, sugar, and vanilla in a medium mixing bowl and mix well to combine. Refrigerate until ready to serve. Cut the strawberries in half and place them in individual serving bowls. Add a few spoonfuls of the cheese mixture on top of the strawberries, sprinkle with the walnut-chocolate mixture, and serve.

Yield: 4 servings

—*Karen's Cucina*

Per serving: 363 Cal.; 48 GI; 21g Prot.; 41g Carb.; 5g SFA; 3g MUFA; 4g PUFA; 1g Omega-3; 286mg Calc.; 233mg Sod.; 592mg Pot.; 1mg Iron; 0mg Phytoestrogen; 4g Fiber

What happens to your weight when you eat too much candy?

It goes up, right? That's because candy has a lot of sugar and almost no nutrients that your body needs to stay healthy and strong. Want an easy way to lose weight? Stop drinking soda and other sweetened drinks.

peaches in wine

Peaches in red wine are a great simple summer dessert after you've enjoyed a fabulous meal.

In a large saucepan, bring the water to a boil. Add the peaches and boil for 15 seconds, and then remove them from the heat and let cool. When cool enough to handle, peel off the skins and remove the pits. Then cut the peaches into ¼-inch slices and set aside.

Put the wine, sugar, cinnamon, and cloves into a medium saucepan and cook over medium heat for 10 minutes, until it reduces to a light syrup. Remove from the heat and let cool.

Place the sliced peaches in 4 wine glasses, then pour the syrup over them and garnish with the sprigs of mint. Serve immediately.

Yield: 4 servings

—*Karen's Cucina*

Per serving: 237 Cal.; 48 GI; 2g Prot.; 49g Carb.; 0g SFA; 0.1g MUFA; 0.2g PUFA; 0g Omega-3; 27mg Calc.; 3mg Sod.; 509mg Pot.; 1mg Iron; 0mg Phytoestrogen; 4g Fiber

2 quarts water

6 ripe yellow peaches

1 cup Chianti wine

½ cup sugar

1 teaspoon ground cinnamon

½ teaspoon ground cloves

4 sprigs of mint

honey-poached pears with citrus biscotti

 Enjoy this delicious dessert for the perfect end to your favorite meal.

BISCOTTI:

2¾ cups whole-wheat flour

1 2/3 cups sugar

1 teaspoon baking powder

½ teaspoon kosher salt

1 large egg

3 large egg yolks

2 teaspoons vanilla extract

2 tablespoons zest (lemon, lime, or orange)

PEARS:

1½ cups honey

1½ cups dry white wine

1 tablespoon lemon juice

1 cup water

6 Bartlett pears, halved and peeled

To make the biscotti, preheat the oven to 350°F. Line a baking sheet with parchment paper.

Put the flour, sugar, baking powder, and salt into the bowl of a food processor.

In a mixing bowl, whisk together the whole egg, egg yolks, and vanilla and add to the dry ingredients in the processor. Mix on low speed, stopping to scrape the bowl occasionally. Add the zest and mix to combine, and then turn the batter out onto a floured work surface and shape it into a long, flattish log. Place the log on the prepared baking sheet pan and bake the biscotti for 5 to 10 minutes, until it is a light golden color and feels firm to the touch. Let cool for 45 minutes.

Preheat the oven to 300°F. Cut the biscotti into ¼-inch slices and lay them on their side on the baking sheet and bake for about 15 minutes, or until they begin to dry. Remove from the oven to cool slightly, and then test for crispness. If necessary return the biscotti to the oven for a few more minutes until they are crisp. Let cool completely and store in an airtight container or Ziploc bags.

To make the pears, place the honey, wine, lemon juice, and water in a non-corrosive saucepan and bring to a boil over medium-high heat. Add the pears, lower the heat to a simmer, and poach the pears until tender, about 8 minutes and up to 25 minutes, depending on how ripe the pears are. When tender, remove from the heat and let cool in the poaching liquid.

When cool, remove the pears with a slotted spoon from the poaching liquid and set aside. Place the saucepan over medium-high heat and cook the poaching liquid until it is reduced to a syrup. Remove from the heat and set aside at room temperature.

To serve, place 2 pear halves in 6 individual serving dishes. Pour each with some of the syrup, and serve with the biscotti on the side.

Yield: 6 servings

—*Gordon Hamersley and Kristin Wilson*

Per serving: 608 Cal.; 66 GI; 11g Prot.; 140g Carb.; 1g SFA; 1g MUFA; 1g PUFA; 0g Omega-3; 107mg Calc.; 629mg Sod.; 559mg Pot.; 3mg Iron; 0mg Phytoestrogen; 12g Fiber

baked apples

This is a very simple and fast recipe that will impress the book club or whomever you have over. It really tastes delicious, has not too many calories, and is the perfect ending to any meal. It's one of my favorite desserts.

4 apples (Rome or Cortland)

¼ cup raisins or cranberries

¼ cup chopped walnuts

½ cup orange juice

¼ teaspoon ground cinnamon

Preheat the oven to 350°F.

Core the apples and place upright in a medium Pyrex baking dish. Combine the raisins and walnuts and fill the cored openings with the mixture. Pour 2 tablespoons of the orange juice into each of the openings. Place in the oven and bake for 45 minutes, or until the apples are easily pierced with the tip of a knife. Cool and serve.

Variations:
- Refrigerate and serve cold.
- Sprinkle with cinnamon before serving.
- Garnish with a dollop of non-fat whipped cream.

Yield: 4 servings

—*Dr. Mache's Kitchen*

Per serving: 185 Cal.; 45 GI; 2g Prot.; 36g Carb.; 0.5g SFA; 1g MUFA; 3g PUFA; 1g Omega-3; 27mg Calc.; 4mg Sod.; 353mg Pot.; 1mg Iron; 0mg Phytoestrogen; 5g Fiber

baked spiced pears with zabaglione sauce

 Pears with cinnamon and cardamom are a marriage made in culinary heaven says *Good Carbs, Bad Carbs* author Johanna Burani. This full-bodied dessert relies exclusively on the wholesome flavors of its ingredients and not added fats, making it an excellent finish to a hearty holiday meal—or even Christmas dinner.

Preheat the oven to 350°F.

Peel, halve, and core the pears. Place them cut side down in a rectangular baking dish with just enough water to cover the bottom of the dish.

Combine the sugar with the spices and sprinkle half of this mixture over the pears. Bake the pears for 5 minutes in the preheated oven. Turn the pear halves over, sprinkle with the remaining sugar-spice mixture, and continue to bake for another 5 minutes. The pears are done when they are easily pierced by a fork but still hold their shape. Large pears may take a little longer to cook. Remove from the oven, place in individual dessert dishes, and set aside.

To make the sauce, combine the egg yolk and sugar in a very small saucepan and mix vigorously for at least 5 minutes with a wooden spoon. Slowly add the marsala and mix well. Heat over low heat, stirring constantly, for approximately 1 minute, or until the mixture thickens. Do not let it come to a boil. Pour the sauce over the pear halves and serve warm or at room temperature.

Yield: 4 servings

—*The University of Sydney Glycemic Index and GI Database*

Per serving: 99 Cal.; 44 GI; 1g Prot.; 18g Carb.; 0g SFA; 0g MUFA; 0g PUFA; 0g Omega-3; 13mg Calc.; 3mg Sod.; 117mg Pot.; 0mg Iron; 0mg Phytoestrogen; 3g Fiber

2 ripe Bosc pears

1 tablespoons LoGiCane sugar

¼ teaspoon ground cinnamon

¼ teaspoon ground cardamom

SAUCE:

1 egg yolk

1 tablespoon LoGiCane sugar

2 tablespoons marsala wine

watermelon granita

When you're too hot to handle, try relaxing and enjoy this cooling, refreshing frozen dessert. Also called "Italian Ice," granitas can also be made with other fruits, such as lemon, pink grapefruit, and strawberries.

SIMPLE SYRUP:

1 cup water

1 cup sugar

GRANITA:

4 cups seedless watermelon chunks

1 cup simple syrup (above)

Juice of 1 lemon

To make the simple syrup, bring the water to a boil in a saucepan. Add the sugar and cook until dissolved. Once the sugar is dissolved completely, remove the saucepan from the heat and set aside to cool fully.

To make the granita, combine the watermelon, simple syrup, and lemon juice in a food processor. Purée until smooth. Pour into a 9 by 13-inch plastic or glass container and freeze for 1 hour. Rake the mixture with a fork and freeze for another hour. Check it a few times to make sure it does not freeze completely. Rake and freeze for 1 more hour. Rake and serve in cups. (The texture should be granular.)

Yield: 4 servings

—*Rachel Giblin*

Per serving: 147 Cal.; 64 GI; 1g Prot.; 37g Carb.; 0g SFA; 0g MUFA; 0g PUFA; 0g Omega-3; 16mg Calc.; 3mg Sod.; 191mg Pot.; 4mg Iron; 0mg Phytoestrogen; 1g Fiber

fruit flambé over sorbet

 This is a great dessert for a party because it's fast and the guests will love the show. It's a nice light dessert that everyone will love, and it's somewhat guiltless.

Put the bananas, strawberries, and agave syrup in a saucepan over medium-low heat and cook for about 1 minute. Remove the pan from the heat and pour in the Grand Marnier. (When you replace the pan on the heat, be prepared for the alcohol to ignite and flame up for a second. Stand back so you don't burn your hair or clothing.) Reduce the heat to low and carefully place the saucepan back on the heat and cook until the fruit is tender but not mushy. Scoop the sorbet, swirl, or ice cream into 6 individual serving bowls and pour the fruit mixture over top. Serve immediately. This is very easy but so yummy!

Yield: 4 servings

—*Will Greenwood*

Per serving: 291 Cal.; 67 GI; 1g Prot.; 64g Carb.; 0g SFA; 0g MUFA; 0.1g PUFA; 0g Omega-3; 27mg Calc.; 12mg Sod.; 332mg Pot.; 1mg Iron; 0mg Phytoestrogen; 3 g Fiber

2 bananas, cut into ½-inch slices

½ pint strawberries, quartered

¼ cup agave syrup

1/3 cup Grand Marnier or Malibu coconut rum

6 scoops of raspberry sorbet, three-flavored swirl, or low-fat vanilla ice cream

baked alaska 2009

 This is a festive traditional dessert that can be served low in fat with low-fat ice cream. It is fun to serve and can be made ahead of time. What more could you ask?

SWISS MERINGUE:

5 egg whites

½ cup agave syrup

CAKE:

1 (½-gallon) container of your favorite sorbet or low-fat ice cream

Angel food cake either purchased or made ahead of time (a cake mix works well)

To make the meringue, take the eggs out of the refrigerator for 45 minutes to come to room temperature. Separate the yolk from the white, making sure there is no yolk at all in the whites (any fat or oil will prevent the meringue from forming). Put the egg whites and agave syrup in a mixing bowl. Place a medium-sized pot of hot water on the stove over medium heat and place the mixing bowl over the pot and whip constantly until the egg whites are warm to the touch, about 110 to 120°F. You may need to adjust the heat; if it is too high, you may cook the whites.

To make the cake, take the ice cream or sorbet out of the freezer to soften it slightly. When the whites and syrup are warmed through, add to a Hobart mixer and whip on high speed until you have a very thick meringue. Set aside.

Cut the cake into the shape of the serving plate you will use to form a base about ¼ inch thick or slightly thicker. (This can have seams and be pieced together as nobody will see it.) Add a layer of the sorbet or ice cream about 5 inches thick on top of this base. With the remaining cake, cut pieces to form a layer about ¼ inch thick on top of the sorbet or ice cream.

Fill a piping bag with the meringue and, using a small knife, ice the cake with the meringue, allowing peaks and spikes to form, because this will make it beautiful when it is heated and browned. You can pipe decorations around the base and on the cake if you like. Have fun making it with the kids because there are no mistakes with baked Alaska.

After the cake is iced, place it in the freezer for at least 4 to 5 hours before serving. You can make this up to 4 days ahead of time or more. The cake needs to be very solid in order to brown it. Restaurants use torches, but a broiler or even the oven will work well. If a torch is used, which is the easiest way, take the cake out about 15 to 20 minutes before serving to temper the ice cream. Light the torch and go over the entire cake, browning everything that has a peak. If the broiler is used, temper it the same, but put it under the broiler, watching carefully that you rotate it and don't let any part burn. This is hardest way to do it. The second easiest way is in the oven. Preheat the oven to 450°F for 20 minutes, and then take the cake directly from the freezer and place it in the oven and bake until it is browned all over. If this method is used, you should not make the peaks so high. (You can use a star-shaped tip for decorating so that there are not any large peaks to burn.) When all the peaks are browned, cut the cake into serving portions and enjoy this classic updated version of hot and cold bliss.

This recipe can also be formed into individual cakes for each person. They are very easy to make and, really, you can't make a mistake when decorating it, so go have fun and enjoy making and eating this classic dessert!

Yield: 6 servings

—*Will Greenwood*

Per serving: 687 Cal.; 69 GI; 10g Prot.; 167g Carb.; 0g SFA; 0g MUFA; 0.1g PUFA; 0g Omega-3; 38mg Calc.; 817mg Sod.; 348mg Pot.; 2mg Iron; 0mg Phytoestrogen; 1.5g Fiber

frozen berry yogurt

Anneka Manning's frozen yogurt from the *Low GI Family Cookbook* is easy to prepare and perfect for summery desserts. You can refreeze it in single-serving containers in the final step rather than 1 large container if you prefer and have it on hand as an after-school snack.

9 ounces fresh or frozen mixed berries

3 (7-ounce) tubs low-fat vanilla yogurt

2 egg whites

2 tablespoons pure floral honey

Place the berries and yogurt in a food processor and blend until smooth. Transfer to a medium-sized bowl and set aside.

Whisk the egg whites in a clean, dry bowl until stiff peaks form. Add the honey, a tablespoon at a time, whisking well after each addition until thick and glossy. Fold into the berry-yogurt mixture until just combined.

Pour the mixture into an airtight container and place in the freezer for 4 hours, or until frozen. Use a metal spoon to break the frozen yogurt into chunks. Blend again in a food processor until smooth. Return to the airtight container and refreeze for 3 hours, or until frozen. Serve in scoops.

Yield: 6 servings

—The University of Sydney Glycemic Index and GI Database

Per serving: 126 Cal.; 43 GI; 6g Prot.; 23g Carb.; 1g SFA; 0.3g MUFA; 0g PUFA; 0g Omega-3; 178mg Calc.; 85mg Sod.; 302mg Pot.; 0.5mg Iron; 0mg Phytoestrogen; 1g Fiber

mock apple pie

 This recipe will leave your guests wanting more of the best apple pie ever. You may even enjoy not telling them that there aren't any apples in the recipe.

Preheat the oven to 350°F.

Place the zucchini slices in a mixing bowl and sprinkle with the lemon juice. Combine the cinnamon, sugars, and flour in a small bowl and stir into the zucchini mixture.

Place one pie crust in the bottom of a 9-inch pie pan. Spread the zucchini mixture in the pan and dot with the butter, if using. Place the other pie crust on top and seal and flute. Bake for 45 minutes, or until the zucchini is tender and the crust is lightly browned.

Yield: 6 servings (1 pie)

—*Cynthia Niles*

Per serving: 223 Cal.; 63 GI; 2g Prot.; 43g Carb.; 1.5g SFA; 3g MUFA; 1g PUFA; 0.3g Omega-3; 31mg Calc.; 44mg Sod.; 193mg Pot.; 1mg Iron; 0mg Phytoestrogen; 1g Fiber

3 cups zucchini, peeled, seeded, and thinly sliced

3 tablespoons lemon juice

1 teaspoon ground cinnamon

½ cup granulated sugar

½ cup brown sugar

3 tablespoons all-purpose flour

Pastry for one 9-inch double-crusted pie

1 tablespoon butter, cut into small pieces (optional)

Get off the sugar rollercoaster
Avoid sugar blasts such as donuts, sweetened soda, and candy. They send your blood sugar up and down quickly and bring your mood with it. Foods rich in B vitamins, such as beets, Brussels sprouts, and asparagus, may help relieve depression.

chocolate mousse pie

This rich-tasting, luxurious chocolate mousse pie is great for any occasion. For an excellent variation, make it with a combination of chocolate and peanut butter chips.

PIE CRUST:

1 cup spelt flour

¼ cup cocoa powder

¼ cup sucanat

1 teaspoon baking powder

1 teaspoon baking soda

½ cup soymilk

½ cup maple syrup

¼ cup safflower oil

½ cup water

½ teaspoon vanilla extract

¼ teaspoon almond extract

2 tablespoons chocolate chips

MOUSSE:

2¼ cups chocolate chips

1 cup plus 2 tablespoons vanilla soymilk

½ teaspoon cocoa powder

½ teaspoon kuzu

1¼ blocks (20 ounces) silken tofu

¼ cup maple syrup

2 teaspoons vanilla extract

1 teaspoon almond extract

To prepare the pie crust, preheat the oven to 325°F. Mix the flour, cocoa powder, sucanat, baking powder, and baking soda together in a large mixing bowl. In another bowl, combine the soymilk, maple syrup, oil, water, and vanilla and almond extracts. Add the wet ingredients to the flour mixture and stir well to combine. Pour the mixture into a baking pan and bake for 35 minutes. Let cool in the refrigerator for about 1 hour.

Crumble the baked dough and press the crust crumbs into a 9-inch pie dish and sprinkle with the chocolate chips.

To prepare the mousse filling, place the chocolate chips, 1 cup of the soymilk, and the cocoa powder in a bowl. Dissolve the kuzu in the remaining 2 tablespoons of soymilk and add to the mixture. Place the mixture in a double boiler and heat over simmering water on medium heat until melted, stirring occasionally. Transfer to a mixing bowl and let cool slightly.

Place the tofu in a food processor and blend until smooth. Add the maple syrup, vanilla, and almond extracts and blend again. Fold into the chocolate mixture until well blended. Pour the chocolate mixture into the pie crust and chill up to 2 hours or overnight before serving.

Yield: 8 servings (1 pie)

—*Benay Vynerib*

Per serving (mousse): 354 Cal.; 34 GI; 8g Prot.; 40g Carb.; 9g SFA; 5g MUFA; 2g PUFA; 0.1g Omega-3; 94mg Calc.; 55mg Sod.; 469mg Pot.; 5mg Iron; 24mg Phytoestrogen; 4g Fiber

Per serving (crust): 223 Cal.; 59 GI; 5g Prot.; 34g Carb.; 1g SFA; 1.5g MUFA; 5.5g PUFA; 0g Omega-3; 97mg Calc.; 275mg Sod.; 203mg Pot.; 2mg Iron; 2mg Phytoestrogen; 3g Fiber

best carrot cake ever

 This is a delicious cake. But be sure not to go back for seconds until tomorrow so you won't gain weight.

Preheat the oven to 350°F. Grease and flour a 13 by 9 by 2-inch baking pan.

To make the cake, combine the flour, sugar, baking soda, baking powder, salt, and cinnamon in a large mixing bowl and mix well. Make a well in the center of the mixture.

In another bowl, combine the oil, applesauce, egg whites, vanilla, pineapple, and carrots and mix well. Pour this mixture into the well in the center of the dry ingredients and mix until well combined. Once the batter is mixed, fold in the coconut and walnuts and spoon into the prepared baking pan. Bake for 45 minutes, or until the cake springs back when pressed lightly in the center with your fingertip.

To make the cream cheese frosting, while the cake is baking, combine the cheese, butter, sugar, and vanilla in a mixing bowl and mix well, adding a little milk if needed to make a spreadable consistency (you can use a hand mixer if you have one).

When the cake is done, put the pan on a wire rack until the cake cools to room temperature. When cool, carefully turn the cake out onto a serving plate, spread the frosting over top, and serve.

Yield: 12 servings

—*Kristin Denice*

Per serving (cake): 393 Cal.; 55 GI; 6g Prot.; 52g Carb.; 5g SFA; 7g MUFA; 7g PUFA; 2g Omega-3; 55mg Calc.; 373mg Sod.; 267mg Pot.; 1.5mg Iron; 0mg Phytoestrogen; 5g Fiber

Per serving (frosting): 151 Cal.; 59 GI; 1.5g Prot.; 21g Carb.; 4g SFA; 1g MUFA; 0g PUFA; 0g Omega-3; 29mg Calc.; 116mg Sod.; 49mg Pot.; 0mg Iron; 0mg Phytoestrogen; 0g Fiber

CAKE:

2 cups whole-wheat flour

1¾ cups sugar

2 teaspoons baking soda

1 teaspoon baking powder

1 teaspoon salt

2 teaspoons ground cinnamon

½ cup oil

½ cup applesauce

3 egg whites

1 teaspoon vanilla extract

1 (8-ounce) can crushed pineapple, drained

2 cups shredded carrots

1 cup flaked coconut

1 cup chopped walnuts

CREAM CHEESE FROSTING:

1 (8-ounce) package light cream cheese

¼ cup butter (½ stick), at room temperature

2 cups confectioners' sugar

1½ teaspoons vanilla extract

Splash of milk if needed

dewberry's triple chocolate brownies

 These are delicious but rich treats, so enjoy one and alternate with other desserts, such as berries.

4 ounces unsweetened baker's chocolate

1 stick butter (¼ pound)

½ cup all-purpose flour

½ cup whole-wheat flour

¼ cup milled flaxseed

¼ teaspoon sea salt

1 cup chopped walnuts or pecans

1 cup chopped bittersweet or semisweet chocolate chips

2 cups granulated or raw sugar

2 tablespoons Ghirardelli sweet ground chocolate and cocoa (or plain cocoa powder)

4 eggs

1 teaspoon vanilla extract

Preheat the oven to 325°F. Line a 9 by 13 by 2-inch baking pan with parchment paper or waxed paper.

In a heavy saucepan, melt the baker's chocolate and butter. Set aside to cool for at least 10 minutes.

Put the flours, milled flaxseed, and salt in a mixing bowl and mix well. Put the nuts and chocolate chips in another bowl and add a tablespoon of the flour mixture. Toss well to coat.

Put the sugar and cocoa powder in a large mixing bowl and add the eggs, one at a time, whisking to mix, but do not overmix. Stir in the vanilla. When the chocolate and butter mixture has cooled, add it to the egg mixture and mix well. Add the flour mixture and mix well, and then fold in the chocolate chips and nuts.

Spread the batter in the prepared pan and bake for 30 to 35 minutes, or until a toothpick comes out mostly clean. If you cook it until the center is completely cooked, it will be overdone and dry.

Cool in the pan for an hour. Run a knife around the edge and turn out onto a rack. Transfer to a cutting board, flipping it to the other side, and cut into 12 pieces. The top is going to crack, so be ready for it. That's the charm of these brownies. Crunchy top and chewy center.

Yield: 12 brownies

—*Jeffrey Parker*

Per serving: 458 Cal.; 59 GI; 7g Prot.; 56g Carb.; 12g SFA; 7g MUFA; 6g PUFA; 1.5g Omega-3; 44mg Calc.; 133mg Sod.; 253mg Pot.; 3mg Iron; 0mg Phytoestrogen; 4.5g Fiber

chocolate zucchini bread

 This is a delicious way to use the abundance of zucchini available in the warm weather. This bread freezes well.

Preheat the oven to 350°F. Grease and flour 3 loaf pans.

Combine the flour, sugar, cocoa, baking powder, baking soda, sugar, and cinnamon in a large mixing bowl and mix well. In a separate bowl, combine the eggs, oil, butter, and extracts and mix well. Stir the egg mixture into the dry ingredients until moistened, and then fold in the zucchini and nuts. Pour the mixture into the prepared loaf pans and bake for 70 minutes, or until a toothpick inserted in the center comes out clean. Remove from the oven and let cool for 10 minutes before removing the loaves from the pans.

Yield: 3 loaves, serving 24 (8 servings per loaf)

—Cynthia Niles

Per serving: 323 Cal.; 57 GI; 4g Prot.; 38g Carb.; 3g SFA; 10g MUFA; 5g PUFA; 1.5g Omega-3; 34mg Calc.; 227mg Sod.; 144mg Pot.; 1mg Iron; 0mg Phytoestrogen, 3g Fiber

3 cups whole-wheat flour

3 cups sugar

½ cup baking cocoa

1½ teaspoons baking powder

1½ teaspoons baking soda

1 teaspoon salt

¼ teaspoon ground cinnamon

4 eggs

1½ cups vegetable oil

2 teaspoons butter, melted

1½ teaspoons vanilla extract

1½ teaspoons almond extract

3 cups grated zucchini

1 cup chopped nuts

fresh cranberry muffins

These muffins are pretty special. Good for you and delicious, they are a great breakfast muffin for a traffic-laden commute. If fresh cranberries are out of season, use dried craisins, but the muffin will be a lot sweeter and not nearly as tart.

Raw sugar (optional)

¾ cup all-purpose flour

1/3 cup granulated sugar

2 teaspoons baking powder

¾ teaspoon ground cinnamon

½ teaspoon baking soda

Pinch of salt

1 cup unprocessed miller's wheat bran

½ cup 1% milk

1 egg

2 tablespoons oil

½ cup chopped fresh cranberries

Preheat the oven to 400°F. Line 8 standard muffin tins with paper baking cups. Sprinkle very lightly with raw sugar if desired.

In a medium mixing bowl, combine the flour, granulated sugar, baking powder, baking soda, salt, cinnamon, and wheat bran and mix well. In another bowl, combine the milk, egg, oil, and cranberries and mix well. Make a well in the center of the dry ingredients and pour in the wet ingredients. Mix just until combined, using as few strokes as possible.

Fill the muffin tins about three-quarters full with the batter and bake for 10 to 20 minutes, until a toothpick inserted in the center comes out clean.

Yield: 8 muffins

—*Jeffrey Parker*

Per serving: 100 Cal.; 65 GI; 3g Prot.; 16g Carb.; 0.5g SFA; 2g MUFA; 1g PUFA; 0.3g Omega-3; 96mg Calc.; 281mg Sod.; 128mg Pot.; 1.5mg Iron; 0mg Phytoestrogen; 4g Fiber

mandle-brodt

 There is no doubt in my mind that this is my favorite cookie. It's not too sweet, it lasts forever in a canister, and it's perfect for any occasion. To change the taste, add 1 cup of raisins, ¾ cup of chocolate chips, or ½ cup of chopped walnuts to the dough.

Preheat the oven to 350°F. Spray a cookie sheet with cooking spray.

In a small mixing bowl, beat the eggs and egg white and add the salt, sugar, oil, and extracts. Mix well. Combine the flour and baking powder in a large mixing bowl and mix well, and then add the egg mixture to the flour mixture and mix until completely combined.

Divide the batter into 4 or 5 equal portions and roll into "logs" and flatten slightly. Combine the sugar and cinnamon and spread on a sheet of waxed paper. Roll the logs in the mixture to lightly coat, and then lay them on the prepared cookie sheet about 1 inch apart. Place in the oven and bake for 30 minutes.

Remove from the oven and cut each log into ½-inch slices. Turn the cookies on their side and leave on the cookie sheet. Turn off the oven and return the cookies to oven until the oven is cool.

Yield: About 60 cookies (2 cookies per serving)

—Bubbie's Kitchen

Cooking spray

2 eggs

1 egg white

Pinch of salt

1 cup sugar

¾ cup oil

1 teaspoon vanilla extract

1 teaspoon almond extract

3½ cups whole-wheat flour

3 teaspoons baking powder

2 tablespoons sugar

2 tablespoons ground cinnamon

Per serving: 133 Cal.; 53 GI; 2g Prot.; 18g Carb.; 0.5g SFA; 4g MUFA; 2g PUFA; 0.5g Omega-3; 39mg Calc.; 95mg Sod.; 66mg Pot.; 1mg Iron; 0mg Phytoestrogen; 2g Fiber

oatmeal chocolate chip cookies

 These healthy cookies are made at the juice bar in the Candle Café and Candle 79 in New York City, and they fly out of the restaurant as soon as they are made.

••

1 cup rolled oats

1 cup spelt flour

¼ cup brown rice flour

¼ teaspoon baking soda

¼ teaspoon fine sea salt

¾ cup safflower oil

¼ cup water

1 cup maple syrup

¼ teaspoon vanilla extract

¼ teaspoon almond extract (optional)

1 tablespoon egg replacer

1 cup chocolate chips

Preheat the oven to 350°F.

Combine the oats, flours, baking soda, and salt in a large mixing bowl. Add the oil, water, maple syrup, vanilla and almond extracts, and the egg replacer and stir well to combine. Fold the chocolate chips into the batter.

Spoon tablespoons of batter onto a large baking sheet and space them 3 inches apart. Flatten the batter with the back of a wet spoon. Bake for 10 to 15 minutes, until lightly browned. Remove the cookies from the baking sheet and let cool on wire racks.

Yield: 18 cookies (2 cookies per serving)

—*Benay Vynerib*

Per serving: 288 Cal.; 46 GI; 3g Prot.; 35g Carb.; 3g SFA; 3g MUFA; 8g PUFA; 0g Omega-3; 29mg Calc.; 68mg Sod.; 192mg Pot.; 2mg Iron; 0mg Phytoestrogen; 3g Fiber

strawberry-yogurt shake

 This is a refreshing drink that is healthy and tastes great.

Place the ingredients, in the order listed, into a food processor. Purée at medium speed until thick and smooth.

Yield: 4 servings

—*Dr. Mache's Kitchen*

Per serving: 118 Cal.; 42 GI; 3g Prot.; 26g Carb.; 0.4g SFA; 0.2g MUFA; 0.1g PUFA; 0.05g Omega-3; 112mg Calc.; 34mg Sod.; 426mg Pot.; 1mg Iron; 0mg Phytoestrogen; 4g Fiber

½ cup unsweetened pineapple juice

¾ cup low-fat, plain yogurt

1½ cups frozen, unsweetened strawberries

Coffee, tea, colas, and even dark chocolate contain caffeine.
The body's digestion brings blood into the abdomen, raises body temperature, and voilà, tells the hypothalamus part of the brain to send a signal that causes hot flashes. Eating smaller meals can help reduce the number of hot flashes.

soy smoothie

 This is a delicious breakfast, snack, or dessert that is rich in isoflavones, so it's good for hot flashes and building strong bones.

1 cup vanilla or plain soymilk

1 medium banana

¼ cup fresh or frozen unsweetened strawberries (or ¼ cup fresh or frozen unsweetened peaches) (optional)

5 ice cubes (only if using fresh fruit)

Place all the ingredients in a food processor and process on medium speed for 1 minute, or until smooth. Garnish with a strawberry and serve.

Yield: 2 servings (1 cup each)

—Dr. Mache's Kitchen

Per serving: 129 Cal.; 71 GI; 5g Prot.; 24g Carb.; 0.3g SFA; 0.4g MUFA; 1g PUFA; 0.6g Omega-3; 158mg Calc.; 71mg Sod.; 395mg Pot.; 1.5mg Iron; 14mg Phytoestrogen; 3g Fiber

mango lassi

 This cooling yogurt drink is a great source of dietary fiber and vitamins B6, A, and C, and yogurt is a great source of calcium. It is healthy and very refreshing.

Place the mango slices, yogurt, maple syrup or honey, ice cubes, and rose water in the bowl of a food processor. Process at high speed until well blended. Serve immediately.

Yield: 4 to 6 servings

—*Dr. Mache's Kitchen*

Per serving: 571 Cal.; 47 GI; 5g Prot.; 26g Carb.; 1g SFA; 0.5g MUFA; 0g PUFA; 0g Omega-3; 193mg Calc.; 71mg Sod.; 375mg Pot.; 0.2mg Iron; 0mg Phytoestrogen; 1.5g Fiber

2 medium mangoes (very ripe), peeled and sliced

2 cups low-fat, plain yogurt

2 tablespoons maple syrup or honey

6 ice cubes

8 teaspoons rose water

golden milk

 Golden milk is a delicious hot drink that the yogis believe is good for your joints and spine. They also believe it is a good nightcap and calming for women.

1/8 teaspoon turmeric

¼ cup water

1 cup 1% milk

2 teaspoons raw almond oil

½ teaspoon honey

Put the turmeric and water in a small saucepan and boil for about 8 minutes, until if forms a thick paste. If too much water boils away, add a little more. Meanwhile, in another saucepan, bring the milk and almond oil just to a boil. As soon as it boils, remove it from the heat. Combine the two mixtures in a large mug and stir in the honey to taste. Delicious hot or cold. You can also blend in a food processor until frothy, and add a sprinkle of cinnamon.

Yield: 1 serving

—*Hari Kaur Khalsa*

Per serving: 178 Cal.; 43 GI; 4g Prot.; 7g Carb.; 2g SFA; 10g MUFA; 2g PUFA; 0g Omega-3; 146mg Calc.; 55mg Sod.; 147mg Pot.; 0.1mg Iron; 0mg Phytoestrogen; 0g Fiber

Vitamins and Minerals for a Healthy Diet*

Vitamin/Mineral	Possible Benefits	Dietary Sources	Concerns
Vitamin A (beta-carotene) RDA Women: 4,000 IU Men: 5,000 IU	Essential for normal growth and for eye and skin health. Helps you see at night.	Carrots, dark green leafy vegetables, cantaloupe, and peaches, as well as liver, eggs, milk, and butter. Beta-carotene is converted in the body to vitamin A.	Generally safe up to 10,000 IU daily. May be toxic above 50,000 IU. Doses above 20,000 IU daily during pregnancy may cause birth defects, but not everyone agrees this is so. High dosages may increase the risk of lung cancer in smokers.
Vitamin B6 (pyridoxine) RDA Adults to age 50: 1.3 mg Pregnant women: 2.0 mg Women over 50: 1.5 mg Men over 50: 1.7 mg	Helps the body process fats, proteins, and carbohydrates, as well as build red blood cells and the immune system. May help prevent heart disease. Women in the United States consume less than the RDA.	Meats, liver, enriched grains, eggs, bananas, and peanut butter.	Dosages above 200 mg daily for several months could lead to numbness in the hands and feet and difficulty walking.
Vitamin B12 (Cyanocobalamin) RDA Adults: 2.4 mcg Pregnant women: 2.6 mcg	Essential for normal cell development, especially blood cells, and protein synthesis. Helps the body use fats and carbohydrates and helps the nervous system work properly.	Meat, fish, eggs, chicken, and dairy products.	Generally without risk in dosages up to 100 mcg. Individuals with abnormal intestinal absorption and strict vegetarians may become B12 deficient during pregnancy, especially if they breast-feed.

Vitamin/Mineral	Possible Benefits	Dietary Sources	Concerns
Vitamin C RDA Adults: 60 mg	Antioxidant, protects cells from natural deterioration that results from aging. Also necessary to produce collagen, which makes up connective tissue.	Fresh fruits (especially citrus) and vegetables, green vegetables, tomatoes, and potatoes.	Dosages up to 1,000 mg probably without risk. Higher dosages may cause diarrhea. Drying, salting, or cooking (especially in copper pots), mincing of fresh vegetables, or mashing potatoes reduces the amount of vitamin C in foods. Pregnant women, smokers, and excessive alcohol consumers benefit from extra vitamin C.
Vitamin D RDA Adults to age 50: 200 IU Adults 51–70: 400 IU Adults over 70: 600–800 IU	Important regulator of the repair and formation of bone. Also controls calcium and phosphorous absorption from food.	Milk is the most important source. Exposure to at least 15 minutes of sunlight without a sunscreen also allows your body to form vitamin D. Older men and women and people living in areas where the days are short probably need a daily supplement of vitamin D.	Dosages up to 2,000 IU are safe. More than 5,000 IU daily can lead to kidney damage unless you are deficient. People in nursing homes or who do not get outside, and women in menopause and with osteoporosis should consider supplementing with vitamin D.
Vitamin E RDA Adults: 30 IU	Antioxidant that protects cells from natural deterioration. Helps reduce risk of heart disease and blood clots. Involved in making red blood cells.	Richest sources include salad dressing, cooking oils, and margarine, which together provide 30% of vitamin E in the American diet. Other sources include almonds, filberts, Brazil nuts, wheat-germ oil, sunflower seeds, corn, asparagus, avocados, organ meats, butter, and eggs.	Studies have shown safety at doses of 800 IU daily. Dosages of at least 100 IU daily appear to have a major potential to reduce the risk of heart attack.

Vitamin/Mineral	Possible Benefits	Dietary Sources	Concerns
Folic Acid RDA Adults: 400 mcg Pregnant women: up to 800 mcg	Helps reduce the risk of heart disease. Helps reduce women's risk of having a baby with a neurological birth defect. Needed for normal red blood cell development.	Raw leafy green vegetables, peas and beans, citrus fruits, and fortified cereals.	The average American consumes only 200 mcg of folic acid daily, and cooking removes more than half of the folic acid in food. Pregnant women with a history of miscarriage or of preeclampsia (a type of high blood pressure in pregnancy), or who take antiseizure medications may benefit from 800 mcg daily. More than 1,000 mcg daily may cause zinc loss or mask B12 deficiency.
Niacin (B3) RDA Women: 14 mg Pregnant women: 18 mg Men: 16 mg	Helps process fat, produce blood sugar, and get rid of waste materials from tissue. Niacin also helps reduce blood cholesterol levels, which reduces the risk of heart disease.	Can be found in meats, but can also be made in the body from the proteins found in eggs and milk. Often added to the flour in breads and pasta.	Safe up to 35 mg daily. Niacin supplements can cause itching, tingling, rashes, and occasionally a feeling of intense heat. Very high dosages of niacin can cause liver damage.
Iron RDA Women: 15 mg Men: 10 mg Pregnant women: 30 mg	Necessary for making red blood cells and hemoglobin.	Abundant in meats, eggs, lentils, nuts, leafy green vegetables, chedder cheese, and muscles.	Believed safe up to 75 mg daily. Needs to be reduced drastically in menopause. Absorption of iron may interfere with absorption of zinc, copper, and calcium. When taking supplemental iron, add 15 mg of zinc and 2 mg of copper. Insufficient iron is a common cause of anemia, especially in children and women of reproductive age due to poor dietary intake.

Vitamin/Mineral	Possible Benefits	Dietary Sources	Concerns
Calcium RDA Children/Young adults: 1–10 yrs: 800–1,200 mg 11–24 yrs: 1,200–1,500 mg Adult women: Pregnant/lactating: 1,200–1,500 mg 25–49 yrs: 1,000 mg 50–64 yrs. taking estrogen: 1,000 mg 50–64 yrs. not on estrogen: 1,500 mg 65+ yrs.: 1,500 mg Adult men 25–64yrs.: 1,000 mg 65+ yrs.: 1,500 mg	Promotes healthy bones, prevents osteoporosis, and helps keep teeth strong. Also essential for muscle contraction and relaxation.	Milk, cheese, yogurt, leafy greens, broccoli, tofu, sardines (especially with bones), and salmon. If you don't eat much of these foods or are lactose intolerant, take a supplement.	Safe up to 2,500 mg daily. May reduce absorption of zinc and iron. Higher dosages can cause kidney stones, so be sure to drink 8 glasses of water daily. The mineral calcium is combined with one of several salts when taken as a supplement. These include calcium carbonate, calcium citrate, and calcium phosphate. Calcium carbonate is the least expensive but is less well absorbed. Calcium citrate and phosphate are absorbed more readily.
Chromium RDA Adults: 50–200 mcg	Helps convert blood sugar into energy. Helps insulin work effectively, so may help prevent diabetes.	Healthy amounts found in peanuts and beer, cheese, broccoli, wheat germ, and liver.	Not recommended above 200 mcg daily.
Zinc RDA Women: 12 mg Men: 15 mg	Helps red blood cells carry carbon dioxide to the lungs for disposal. Helps wound healing and keeping the senses alert. May help prevent colds and reduce risk of premature delivery toward the end of pregnancy.	Abundant in red meats, bread and other grain products, eggs, milk, sunflower seeds, soybeans, chicken, and seafood (especially oysters).	Safe up to 30 mg daily. 2,000 mg daily can lead to vomiting.

*From Seibel MM, Khalsa HK. A woman's book of yoga. New York: Penguin Putnam; 2002.

Aldo, Chef
Riverside Country Club
2500 Springhill Road
Bozeman, MT 59718
Tel.: 406-587-5105

Antonio Laudisio
Laudisio Italian Restaurant
1710 29th Street
Boulder, CO 80301

Aviva Goldfarb
The Six O'Clock Scramble
Chevy Chase, MD
www.thescramble.com

Benay Vynerib, COO
Candle Café and Candle 79
1307 Third Avenue
New York, NY 10021-3301
Tel.: 212-472-0970 / 212-537-7179
E-mail: Benay@candlecafe.com
www.candlecafe.com

Ben Schwendener
Gravity Arts Studio
Jamaica Plain, MA
www.BenSchwendener.com

Bill Hart, Chef
Black Dog Café
Martha's Vineyard, MA

Brad Parsons, Chef
Fairmont Chicago, Millennium
Park
200 North Columbus Drive
Chicago, IL 60601

Brad Stevens, Executive Chef
Community Servings
Jamaica Plain, MA
Tel.: 617-522-7777
www.servings.org

Bubbie's Kitchen (Elaine Seibel)
Houston, TX

Carrie Nahabedian
NAHA Restaurant, Chicago
500 North Clark Street
Chicago, IL 60654
Tel.: 312-321-6242

Catherine D'Amato
Greater Boston Food Bank
70 South Bay Avenue
Boston, MA 02118

Cathy Whims, Chef
Nostrana
1401 SE Morrison
Portland, OR 97214
E-mail: nostrana@gmail.com

Cynthia Niles
Red Hot Mamas
Charlestown, RI

Donnie Ferneau Jr., CEC
Ferneau Restaurant
2601 Kavanaugh Blvd.
Little Rock, AR 72205
Tel.: 501-603-9208
www.ferneaurestaurant.com

Dr. Mache's Kitchen
(Mache Seibel)

Gordon Hamersley
Hamersley's Bistro
553 Tremont Street
Boston, MA 02118
E-mail: Ghamersley3@aol.com

Hari Kaur Khalsa
New York, NY
www.reachhari.com

Heather Tsatsarones, MS, RD, LDN
Community Servings
Jamaica Plain, MA
Tel.: 617-522-7777
www.servings.org

Jason Franey, Chef
Canlis Restaurant
2576 Aurora Avenue North
Seattle, WA 98109
Tel: 206-283-3313
www.canlis.com

Jeffrey S. Merry, Chef
Agar Supply
225 John Hancock Road
Taunton, MA 02780-7318
Tel.: 617-880-5164
E-mail: jmerry@agarsupply.com

Jeffrey Parker
Former contestant on *Hell's Kitchen*
The Flying Biscuit Cafe
Atlanta, GA
www.flyingbiscuit.com

Joanne Choi
Week of Menus
www.weekofmenus.com

John Liberatore
Liberatore's Restaurant
9515 Deereco Road
Timonium, MD 21093
Tel: 410-561-3300
Fax: 410-561-240

Jonathan Cartwright, Chef
The White Barn Inn
37 Beach Avenue
Kennebunk Beach, ME 04043
E-mail: jonathan.cartwright@
ushotelsgroup.com

Karen's Cucina
(Karen Giblin)

Kristin Denice
Narragansett, RI

Kristin Wilson
Hamersley's Bistro
553 Tremont Street
Boston, MA 02118

Luis Bollo, Chef
Meigas Restaurant
10 Wall Street
Norwalk, CT 06850
Tel.: 203-866-8800
Contact: Mario Aguilar
E-mail: m2a2forever@yahoo.com

Michael Fiorello, Chef de Cuisine
Mercat à la Planxa
638 South Michigan Avenue
Chicago, IL 60605
www.mercatchicago.com

Michelle Bernstein
Michy's
6927 Biscayne Blvd.
Miami, FL 33138
Tel.: 305-759-2001

Neal Fraser, Chef
Grace Restaurant
7360 Beverly Blvd.
Los Angeles, CA 90036-2501
E-mail: neal@gracerestaurant.com

Rachel Giblin
Red Hot Mamas
Bozeman, MT

Tony Murillo, Kitchen Manager
Community Servings
Jamaica Plain, MA
Tel.: 617-522-7777
www.servings.org

Tres Hundertmark, Chef
The Lobster Trap
35 Patton Avenue
Asheville, NC 28801
Tel.: 828-350-0505
E-mail: tres@thelobstertrap.biz

University of Sydney Glycemic
Index and GI Database
Sydney, Australia
www.glycemicindex.com

Will Greenwood, Chef Consultant
E-mail: Chefgreenwood@aol.com
www.myspace.com/chefwill
greenwood.com

Index to Recipes

Note: The letter *b* following a page number indicates that the recipe is in a box on that page.

Index to Nutritional Information